SIMPLE 2

MORE OF
THE EASIEST
RECIPES
IN THE WORLD

JEAN-FRANÇOIS MALLET

BLACK DOG
& LEVENTHAL
PUBLISHERS
NEW YORK

Introduction: All New Recipes

This new book comes in response to the question I have been asked every day since the success of the other Simple cookbooks: "We loved your first cookbook. When are you going to publish more recipes for everyday meals?"

Creating new recipes that appeal to everyone and that require only a few ingredients found in everyone's refrigerator or pantry can really make your head spin! But in this second cookbook, I have once again accomplished just that.

Here I have created *new* fast and easy recipes for every day that will appeal to all tastes. I even offer some essential dessert recipes (as published in my cookbook *Simple Desserts: The Easiest Recipes in the World*), such as Decadent Chocolate Cake, Crème Caramel, and Classic Tiramisu. With the right combinations of flavors and simple ingredients, it's possible to make great—even impressive—food without spending hours in the kitchen.

Once again, the recipes are about simplicity: a maximum of six ingredients per recipe, each presented in photos, with just a few lines of instructions—all you have to do is perform a few easy steps and it's ready!

I wish you happiness in the kitchen . . . and especially at the table. *Bon appétit*!

CONTENTS

INSTRUCTIONS

For successful results with these recipes, all you need is:

- Running water
- A stove
- A refrigerator
- A skillet
- A cast-iron pot
- A sharp knife
- A pair of scissors
- Salt and pepper
- Oil: both extra-virgin olive oil and flavorless cooking oil

(If you do not have all of these items, this is a great time to make a small investment!)

What essential ingredients should you have?

- **Canned foods:** Tuna and sardines packed in oil, coconut milk, and the indispensable jar of tomato sauce or crushed tomatoes.
- **Herbs:** Fresh herbs have no equal when it comes to adding flavor, so it's important to buy fresh whenever possible. But in case of "emergencies" when fresh herbs are not available, you can always use frozen or dried herbs (although their flavors will not be as good).
- **Vegetables and fruits:** These should be purchased fresh and in season whenever possible but do not hesitate to buy frozen, if necessary. For citrus fruit, I recommend organic, which is always better, especially when you are using the zest. Wash all fruits and vegetables before using.
- **Oils:** Olive oil (extra-virgin is always best), sesame, and walnut or hazelnut oils—just a drizzle of one of these can really enhance a dish or change the seasoning of a salad.
- **Spices:** These are simple to use and can give your dishes a little exotic or modern touch that will really impress your guests. Try to always have curry powder, caraway seeds, saffron threads, and paprika on hand.
- **Pasta:** Do not hesitate to change the type of pasta used in the recipes to suit your taste (and according to what you have on hand in your pantry).
- **Condiments:** I always have mustard, pesto, tapenade, and soy sauce on hand. These can often pep up a dish in a jiffy. As for soy sauce, it's preferable to use Japanese, such as Kikkoman brand (the one with the green cap) as it's less salty.

What basic cooking methods should you adopt?

Cooking pasta: Cook pasta in a large quantity of boiling salted water in a large saucepan. Watch the cooking time very closely if you prefer your pasta cooked al dente (still slightly firm to the bite).

Using a bain-marie (a water bath): This technique allows you to melt or even cook ingredients without the risk of burning them. To prepare a bain-marie, place the pan containing your preparation over a separate larger pan of boiling water.

Marinating: This means to soak an ingredient in an aromatic preparation to create more flavor or to tenderize it.

Beating egg whites: Add a pinch of salt to egg whites and use an electric mixer to beat them, gradually increasing the mixer speed as the whites increase in volume. Always beat the egg whites in the same direction (clockwise or counterclockwise) to avoid breaking them.

Whipping cream: To successfully whip cream, the cream and the bowl must be very cold (place the bowl in the freezer a few minutes before whipping). Use an electric mixer and select the proper whipping cream (one with a sufficiently high fat content) so that it will whip; a low-fat cream will never whip.

Reducing a liquid: Reduce the volume of a liquid through evaporation by keeping it boiling while uncovered. Creating a reduction concentrates flavors and creates a silky texture.

Zesting citrus fruit: There are three ways to zest citrus fruit: For a very fine zest, a cheese grater works great. Scrape each spot on the fruit against the grater only once to avoid the white, bitter membrane underneath. But the best investment is a Microplane grater, found in any kitchen store, which will produce perfect fine zest each time. For long strips of zest that look like vermicelli, use a zester. For wide strips, use a vegetable peeler.

What appliances should you have?

Electric standing or handheld mixer: This is the perfect tool for quickly beating egg whites to stiff peaks or for whipping cream. A hand whisk will achieve the same result but will require a good amount of elbow grease!

Immersion blender: This tool is used to mix and purée liquid mixtures such as fruit-based soups, smoothies, and milk shakes. An immersion blender is easy to use, inexpensive, and space saving. It also cuts down on cleanup because it is used directly in the saucepan or pot in which the mixture is made without having to transfer the contents to a blender.

Blender: Countertop blenders are more expensive and more cumbersome than immersion blenders, but mixtures turn out more smooth and velvety.

What oven temperature setting?

200°F/90°C: thermostat 3

250°F/120°C: thermostat 4

300°F/150°C: thermostat 5

350°F/180°C: thermostat 6

400°F/210°C: thermostat 7

475°F/240°C: thermostat 8

500°F/270°C: thermostat 9

575°F/300°C: thermostat 10

That's it! For everything else, just simply follow the recipes!

SAVORY PALMIERS

Puff pastry dough
x 1 sheet (8 ounces/227 g)

Mustard
1 tbsp (15 mL

Rillettes (pork or duck)
3½ ounces (100 g)

👤 4 to 5

🕐

Preparation time: 10 min.
Refrigeration: 30 min.
Cooking time: 20 min.

- Preheat the oven to 400°F/210°C.
- Unroll the **dough** onto parchment paper. Evenly spread the **mustard** and then the **rillettes** on top. Tightly roll up the **dough** from both sides in toward the center. Refrigerate for 30 minutes to set.
- Cut the log crosswise into ¼-inch (5-mm) -thick slices and place them on a parchment-lined baking sheet. Bake for 20 minutes, or until puffed and golden.

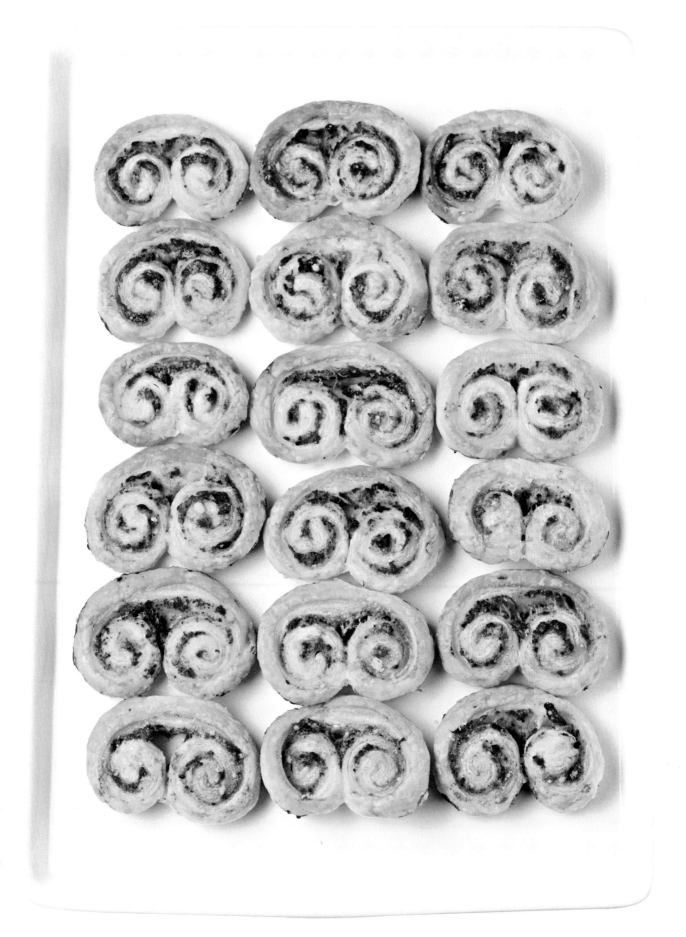

COMTÉ AND CUMIN CRACKERS

Unsalted butter
7 tbsp (3½ ounces/100 g),
at room temperature

All-purpose flour
2 cups (7 ounces/200 g)

Grated Comté cheese
5¼ ounces (150 g)

Cumin seeds
1 tbsp

Preparation time: 10 min.
Refrigeration: 30 min.
Cooking time: 10 min.

- Preheat the oven to 350°F/180°C.
- Combine the **butter**, **flour**, **Comté**, and **cumin seeds** to form a smooth dough. Shape the dough into a long log, wrap it in plastic wrap, and refrigerate for 30 minutes, or until firm.
- Cut the log crosswise into ¼-inch (5-mm) -thick rounds and place them on a parchment-lined baking sheet. Bake for 10 minutes, or until pale golden. Serve warm or cooled.

MACKEREL-IN-MUSTARD DIP

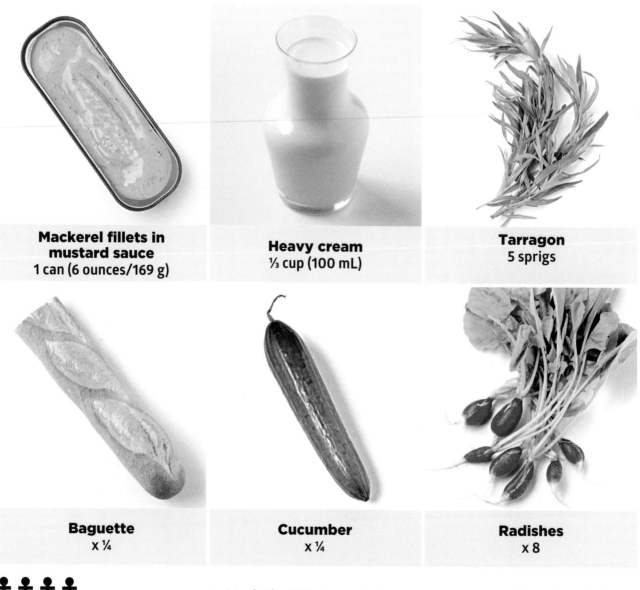

Mackerel fillets in mustard sauce
1 can (6 ounces/169 g)

Heavy cream
⅓ cup (100 mL)

Tarragon
5 sprigs

Baguette
x ¼

Cucumber
x ¼

Radishes
x 8

Preparation time: 5 min.

• Mash the **fillets** in their mustard sauce with a fork. Using an electric mixer, beat the **cream** into soft peaks (do not overbeat) and fold it into the mashed mackerel. Coarsely chop the **tarragon** and fold it into the mixture.

• Slice the **baguette** and **cucumber** into strips. Serve immediately with the **baguette**, **cucumber**, and **radishes** on the side.

GOAT CHEESE PINWHEELS

Fresh goat cheese minilog
x ½

Puff pastry dough
x 1 sheet (8 ounces/227 g)

Dried thyme
1 tbsp

Honey
1 tbsp (15 mL)

👤 4 to 5

🕐

Preparation time: 10 min.
Refrigeration: 30 min.
Cooking time: 20 min.

• Cut the **cheese** into small pieces. Unroll the **dough** onto parchment paper, evenly distribute the **cheese** and **thyme** on top, then drizzle with the **honey**. Tightly roll up the **dough** to form a log. Refrigerate for 30 minutes, or until firm.

• Meanwhile, preheat the oven to 400°F/210°C.

• Cut the log crosswise into ¼-inch (5-mm) -thick slices and place them on a parchment-lined baking sheet. Bake for 20 minutes, or until puffed and golden.

PASTRAMI SPRING ROLLS

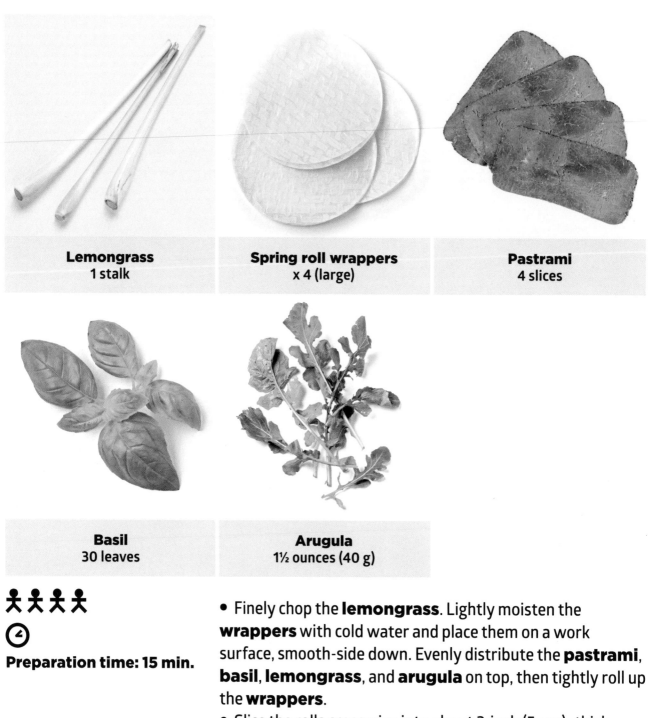

Lemongrass
1 stalk

Spring roll wrappers
x 4 (large)

Pastrami
4 slices

Basil
30 leaves

Arugula
1½ ounces (40 g)

Preparation time: 15 min.

• Finely chop the **lemongrass**. Lightly moisten the **wrappers** with cold water and place them on a work surface, smooth-side down. Evenly distribute the **pastrami**, **basil**, **lemongrass**, and **arugula** on top, then tightly roll up the **wrappers**.

• Slice the rolls crosswise into about 2-inch (5-cm) -thick pieces; serve, with an aperitif.

ROSEMARY BREADSTICKS

Pizza dough
x 1 (about 12 ounces/340 g),
fresh or frozen

Rosemary
2 sprigs

Grated Parmesan cheese
2 tbsp (¼ ounce/6 g)

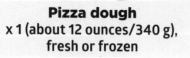

Extra-virgin olive oil
1 tbsp (15 mL)

Preparation time: 10 min.
Cooking time: 10 min.

- Preheat the oven to 350°F/180°C.
- Roll out the **dough** onto parchment paper. Strip the **rosemary** leaves from their stems and chop the leaves. Sprinkle the leaves over the top of the **dough**, then sprinkle on half the **Parmesan**. Shape the **dough** into a ball, then roll it out again into a large circle.
- Cut the **dough** into thin strips and place them on a parchment-lined baking sheet. Sprinkle with the remaining **Parmesan**, then drizzle with the **oil**. Bake for 10 minutes, or until golden and crisp.

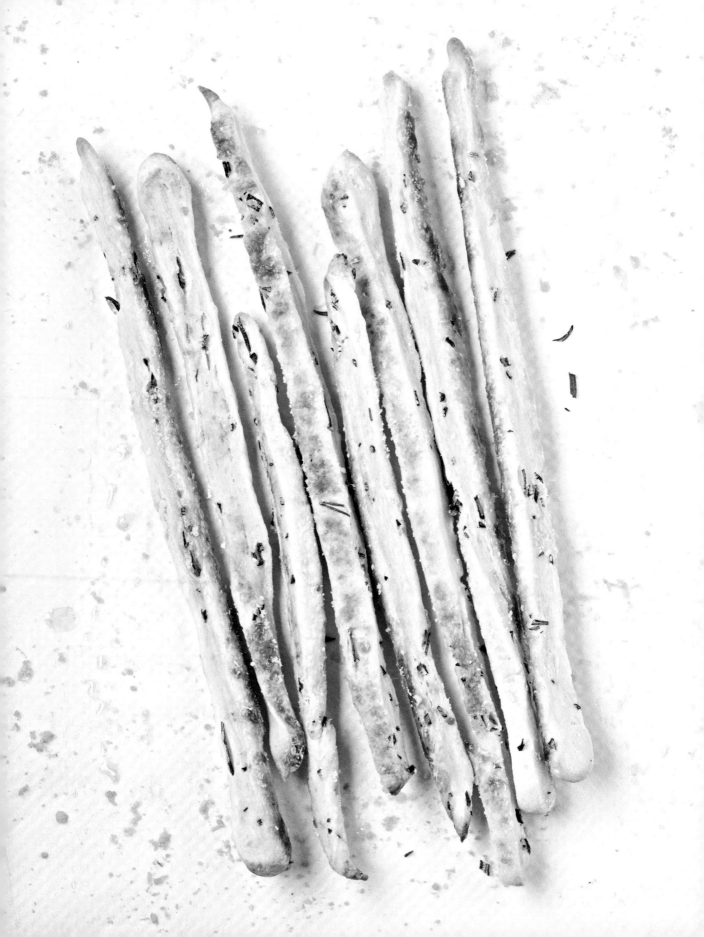

SARDINE AND BASIL SPREAD

Sardines in olive oil
2 cans (about 4 ounces/
113 g each)

Basil
10 leaves

Organic lemon
x 1 (small)

Fromage frais
(or ricotta cheese)
¼ cup (1¾ ounces/50 g)

Baguette
x 16 slices

👤 4 to 5

🕐
Preparation time: 3 min.

• Mash the **sardines** with a fork in half their oil. Finely chop the **basil** leaves and stir them into the mixture. Zest the **lemon** into the mixture, cut it in half, then squeeze in the juice; stir to combine. Stir in the **fromage frais**.

• Serve with the **baguette** slices.

CHORIZO SABLÉS

Chorizo
1¾ ounces (50 g)

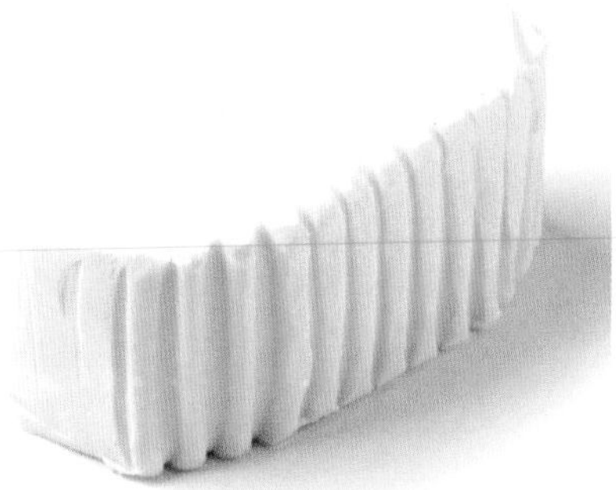

Unsalted butter
7 tbsp (3½ ounces/100 g), at room temperature

All-purpose flour
1 cup (3½ ounces/100 g)

Grated Parmesan cheese
5¼ ounces (150 g)

Preparation time: 10 min.
Refrigeration: 15 min.
Cooking time: 10 min.

- Cut the **chorizo** into small pieces. Combine the **butter**, **flour**, **Parmesan**, and **chorizo** to form a smooth dough. Refrigerate the dough for 15 minutes, or until firm.
- Meanwhile, preheat the oven to 350°F/180°C.
- Slice the dough into ¼-inch (5-mm) -thick rounds, then shape them into small balls. Place them on a parchment-lined baking sheet. Bake for 10 minutes, or until golden. Serve warm or cooled.

PROSCIUTTO AND PARMESAN BITES

Pizza dough
x 1 (about 12 ounces/340 g),
fresh or frozen

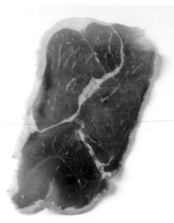

Prosciutto
4 slices

Grated Parmesan cheese
1 tbsp (⅛ ounce/3 g)

Salt, pepper

Preparation time: 10 min.
Cooking time: 10 min.

- Preheat the oven to 350°F/180°C.
- Roll out the **dough** onto parchment paper. Tear the **prosciutto** into small pieces and distribute them on top of the dough; add salt and pepper. Roll up the **dough** from both sides in toward the center, then shape it into a log. Cut ⅓-inch (1-cm) -thick slices and place them on a parchment-lined baking sheet. Sprinkle with the **Parmesan** and bake for 10 minutes, or until golden. Serve warm.

ASPARAGUS TWISTS WITH ORANGE DIP

Asparagus
x 12 spears

Puff pastry dough
x 1 sheet (8 /227 g)

Grated Parmesan cheese
1 tbsp (⅛ ounce/3 g)

Extra-virgin olive oil
4 tbsp (60 mL)

Organic orange
x 1

 4 to 5

Preparation time: 10 min.
Cooking time: 20 min.

- Preheat the oven to 400°F/210°C.
- Cut off and discard the tough stem ends of the **asparagus**.
- Unroll the **dough** onto parchment paper. Cut it into 6 strips, then cut the strips in half. Roll up 1 **asparagus** spear in each. Place them on a parchment-lined baking sheet. Sprinkle with the **Parmesan** and bake for 20 minutes, or until puffed and pale golden.
- Combine the **oil** with the zest and juice of the **orange**. Serve with the orange dipping sauce.

CHICKEN AND OLIVE SPREAD

| **Chicken legs** x 2 | **White wine** Just over ¾ cup (200 mL) | **Dried thyme** 2 tsp |

| **Olive tapenade** 2 tbsp (30 mL) | **Baguette** x 16 slices |

🧍🧍🧍🧍

🧂 Salt, pepper

🫗 1 tbsp (15 mL) flavorless cooking oil

②

Preparation time: 5 min.
Cooking time: 1 hr. 20 min.

- Sear the **chicken legs** in a pan with the oil over high heat for 5 minutes, then add the **wine**, **thyme**, and just over ¾ cup (200 mL) of water. Simmer over low heat, covered, for 1 hour 15 minutes, or until the thighs are cooked through.
- Remove the thighs, pull the meat from the bones, and combine it with the **tapenade** and the cooking juices from the pan. Add salt and pepper, then let cool.
- Serve with the **baguette**, lightly toasted.

OYSTERS WITH FOIE GRAS

Oysters
x 12

Cooked foie gras
2⅛ ounces (60 g)

Coarse-ground peppercorns
1 tsp (3 g)

Balsamic vinegar
2 tbsp (30 mL)

Preparation time: 5 min.
Cooking time: 7 min.

- Preheat the oven to 400°F/210°C.
- In a baking dish, bake the **oysters** for 5 minutes so that they open more easily; open the **oysters**. Place a piece of **foie gras** on top of each **oyster**. Sprinkle with the **peppercorns**, then bake for 2 more minutes.
- Spoon a little **balsamic vinegar** on top and serve immediately.

MICROWAVE SPICED FOIE GRAS

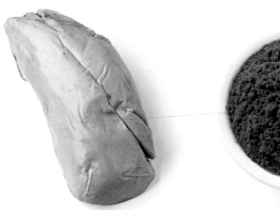

Foie gras
1 lobe (14 ounces/400 g),
raw and deveined

Paprika
1 tbsp

Cognac
2 tbsp (30 mL)

👤👤👤👤

🧂🧂 **Salt, pepper**

🕐

Preparation time: 5 min.
Cooking time: 2 min.
Refrigeration: 12 hr.

• Sprinkle the **foie gras** with salt and pepper. Spread the **paprika** and **cognac** thoroughly over the entire surface of the **foie gras**, then press it into a microwave-safe terrine. Cover the terrine with plastic wrap and microwave for 2 minutes (at 800 watts).
• Refrigerate for 12 hours.
• Serve in thick slices.

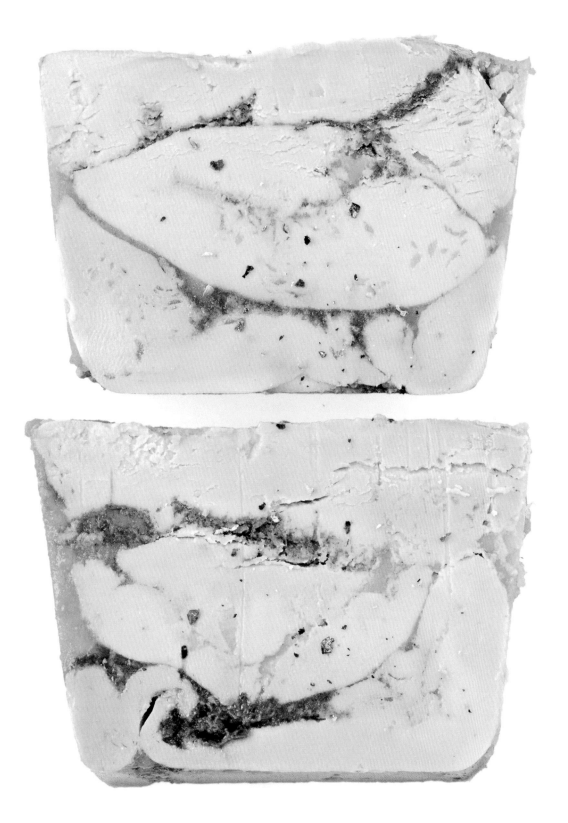

CLAMS WITH RASPBERRY

Clams x 32 (washed well)	**Basil** 32 leaves	**Fresh raspberries** x 16 (halved)

Raspberry vinegar 2 tbsp (30 mL)	**Extra-virgin olive oil** 4 tbsp (60 mL)

👤👤👤👤

🕐

Preparation time: 5 min.
Cooking time: 5 min.

- Cook the **clams** with ⅔ cup (150 mL) of water in a pot over low heat for 5 minutes to open them.
- Remove and discard the top shells and place the **clams** on a large serving plate. Place a **basil** leaf, then a half **raspberry**, on top.
- Combine the **vinegar** with the **oil** and drizzle this mixture on top of the **clams**; serve immediately.

SHRIMP SPRING ROLLS

Cucumber
5¼ ounces/150 g

Peanuts
4 tbsp (1¼ ounces/36 g)

Spring roll wrappers
x 4 (large)

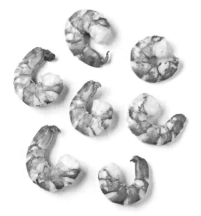

Shrimp
x 12 (cooked and peeled)

Mint
35 leaves (large)

Soy sauce
4 tbsp (60 mL)

Preparation time: 15 min.

- Slice the **cucumber** into thin strips. Crush the **peanuts**.
- Lightly moisten the **spring roll wrappers** with cold water and place them on a work surface, smooth-side down. Place 3 **shrimp**, 5 **cucumber** strips, 1 small spoonful of **peanuts**, and 7 **mint** leaves on top of each. Fold over the ends, then roll them up tightly.
- Chop the remaining **mint** leaves and combine them with the **soy sauce** and any remaining crushed **peanuts**, for dipping.

OYSTERS WITH AVOCADO AND PEPPERCORNS

Oysters
x 8 (medium)

Avocado
x 1 (very ripe)

Lemon
x 1

Cilantro
½ bunch

Pink peppercorns
1 tbsp (⅓ ounce/10 g)

Drizzle of extra-virgin olive oil

Preparation time: 10 min.
Cooking time: 5 min.

- Preheat the oven to 350°F/180°C.
- Bake the **oysters** for 5 minutes so that they open more easily.
- Peel and pit the **avocado**. Scoop out the flesh and mash it with a fork. Halve the **lemon** and squeeze the juice over the avocado, then stir in the **cilantro** leaves.
- Spoon a little of the avocado mixture on top of the **oysters**. Season with the **peppercorns** and a drizzle of oil; serve immediately.

APRICOT-DUCK SPRING ROLLS

Fresh apricots
x 4

Spring roll wrappers
x 4 (large)

Smoked duck breast
12 thin slices

Arugula
1½ ounces (40 g)

👤👤👤👤

🕐

Preparation time: 15 min.

- Cut each **apricot** into 6 wedges.
- Lightly moisten the **spring roll wrappers** with cold water and place them on a work surface, smooth-side down.
- Distribute the **duck breast**, **arugula**, and **apricot** wedges on top of each one and roll them up tightly.
- Serve whole or sliced.

SALMON CEVICHE WITH COCONUT AND BASIL

Salmon fillet
1⅓ lb (600 g), skinless
and boneless

Organic limes
x 2

Coconut milk
Just over ¾ cup (200 mL)

Basil
1 bunch

👤👤👤👤

🧂🧂 **Salt, pepper**

🕐

Preparation time: 10 min.
Marinating: 5 min.

- Cube the **salmon**. Zest and juice the **limes**.
- Marinate the **salmon** for 5 minutes in the **coconut milk** and the **lime** zest and juice.
- Chop the **basil** and stir it into the mixture. Add salt and pepper. Divide among small bowls and serve immediately.

TUNA-BLUEBERRY CARPACCIO

Fresh tuna
14 ounces (400 g)

Extra-virgin olive oil
2 tbsp (30 mL)

Lemon
x 1

Fresh blueberries
1 container (4½ ounces/125 g)

Arugula
1 ounce (30 g)

Salt, pepper

Preparation time: 10 min.
Marinating: 10 min.

• Thinly slice the **tuna**. Combine it with the **oil** and the juice from the **lemon** and let marinate for 10 minutes.

• Arrange the slices on a plate and drizzle them with the marinade. Add the **blueberries** and **arugula** on top. Add salt and pepper; serve.

SALMON CEVICHE WITH PASSION FRUIT

Salmon fillets
x 2 (about 3 ounces/85 g each),
skinless and boneless

Passion fruits
x 4

Extra-virgin olive oil
2 tbsp (30 mL)

Mint
10 leaves

Salt, pepper

Preparation time: 10 min.
Marinating: 5 min.

• Dice the **salmon**. Halve the **passion fruits**, scoop out the pulp, and combine it with the **salmon** and the **oil**. Add salt and pepper and let marinate for 5 minutes.

• Chop the **mint** and stir it into the mixture. Spoon the mixture back into the empty **passion fruit** hulls and serve.

PROSCIUTTO, CANTALOUPE, AND ARUGULA SALAD

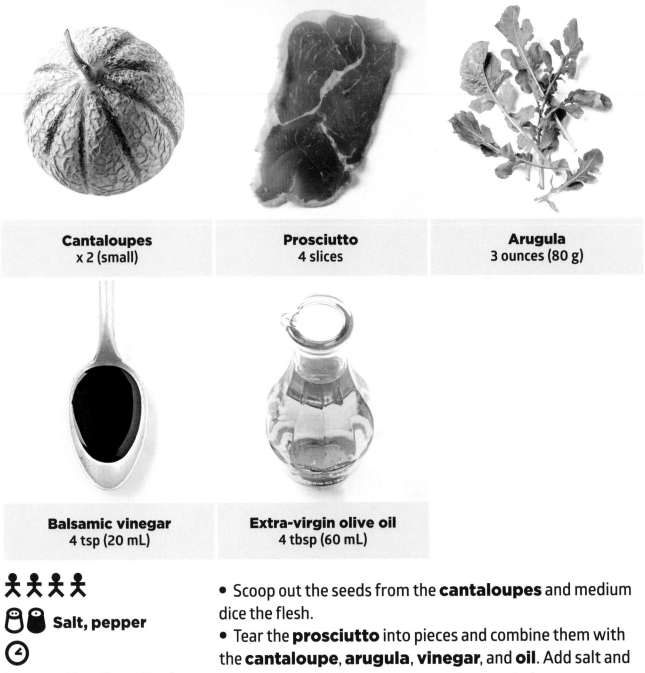

Cantaloupes
x 2 (small)

Prosciutto
4 slices

Arugula
3 ounces (80 g)

Balsamic vinegar
4 tsp (20 mL)

Extra-virgin olive oil
4 tbsp (60 mL)

🧍🧍🧍🧍

🧂🧂 **Salt, pepper**

🕐
Preparation time: 5 min.

• Scoop out the seeds from the **cantaloupes** and medium dice the flesh.

• Tear the **prosciutto** into pieces and combine them with the **cantaloupe**, **arugula**, **vinegar**, and **oil**. Add salt and pepper; serve in the empty **cantaloupe** rinds.

EGGPLANT AND GOAT CHEESE SPREAD

Eggplants
x 2

Fresh goat cheese
5¼ ounces (150 g)

Cilantro
1 bunch

Salt, pepper

Drizzle of extra-virgin olive oil

Preparation time: 5 min.
Cooking time: 40 min.

- Preheat the oven to 350°F/180°C.
- Bake the whole **eggplants** for 40 minutes, or until softened.
- Halve the **eggplants** and scoop out the flesh; let cool slightly.
- Chop the **cheese** and **cilantro**. Mash the **eggplant** flesh with a fork, then stir in the **cheese** until melted and smooth. Add salt and pepper. Add in the **cilantro** and add a drizzle of oil on top. Serve, spread on toasted baguette slices.

TOMATO AND MINT SALAD

Cherry tomatoes
1 container (9 ounces/250 g)

Lemongrass
2 stalks

Mint
2 bunches

Extra-virgin olive oil
4 tbsp (60 mL)

Fried shallots
2 tbsp

Salt, pepper

Preparation time: 10 min.

- Halve the **tomatoes**. Finely chop the **lemongrass**.
- Five minutes before serving, combine the **tomatoes**, **mint** leaves, and **lemongrass** with the **oil**; add salt and pepper.
- Divide among bowls and sprinkle the fried **shallots** on top; serve immediately.

OCTOPUS ANTIPASTO

Small octopuses
x 15

Lemons
x 2

Dried oregano
2 tsp

Caper berries (or use capers)
x 20 (2⅛ ounces/60 g)

Extra-virgin olive oil
½ cup (120 mL)

Preparation time: 5 min.
Cooking time: 15 min.
Marinating: 1 hr.

- Bring a saucepan of salted water to a boil. Add the **octopuses**, reduce the heat to low, and cook for 10 minutes; drain.
- Juice the **lemons**. In a bowl, combine the **lemon** juice, **oregano**, **caper berries**, and **oil** with ⅓ cup (100 mL) of water. Add the **octopuses**, stir, then let marinate for 1 hour; serve.

VIETNAMESE EGG ROLL SALAD

Store-bought pork egg rolls
x 8 (with sauce)

Lemongrass
2 stalks

Arugula
5¼ ounces (150 g)

Mint
2 bunches

Salt, pepper

Preparation time: 5 min.
Cooking time: 25 min.

- Preheat the oven to 400°F/210°C.
- Bake the **egg rolls** for 25 minutes, or until crisp.
- Finely chop the **lemongrass**. While still warm, cut the **egg rolls** into bite-size pieces, then toss them with the **lemongrass**, **arugula**, **mint** leaves, and **egg roll** sauce. Add salt and pepper; serve immediately.

MEXICAN TUNA TARTARE

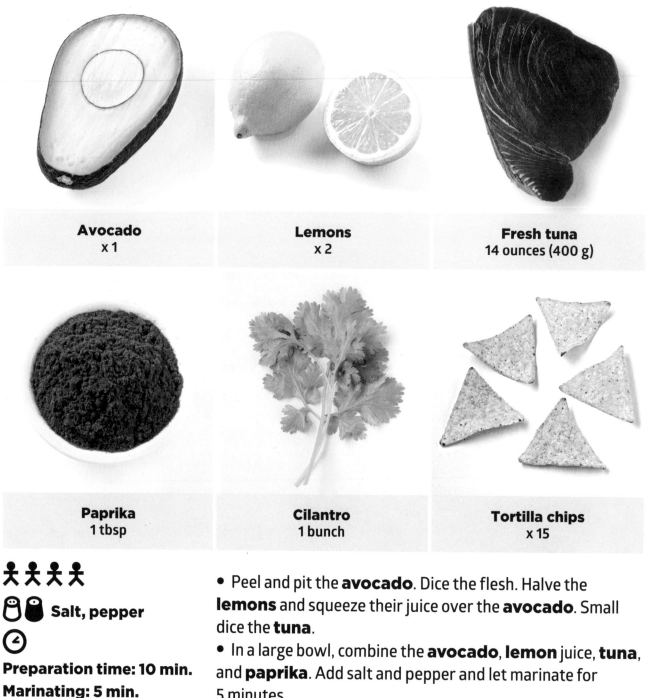

Avocado
x 1

Lemons
x 2

Fresh tuna
14 ounces (400 g)

Paprika
1 tbsp

Cilantro
1 bunch

Tortilla chips
x 15

🏃🏃🏃🏃

🧂🧂 **Salt, pepper**

🕐

Preparation time: 10 min.
Marinating: 5 min.

- Peel and pit the **avocado**. Dice the flesh. Halve the **lemons** and squeeze their juice over the **avocado**. Small dice the **tuna**.
- In a large bowl, combine the **avocado**, **lemon** juice, **tuna**, and **paprika**. Add salt and pepper and let marinate for 5 minutes.
- Add **cilantro** leaves on top, then place the tuna mixture on the **chips**; serve immediately.

STRAWBERRY TABBOULEH

Couscous
1 cup (6 ounces/180 g)

Cucumber
x ½

Fresh strawberries
x 16

Mint
1 bunch

Extra-virgin olive oil
5 tbsp (75 mL)

Salt, pepper

Preparation time: 5 min.
Cooking time: 1 min.

- In a small microwave-safe bowl, combine the **couscous** with 2 cups (500 mL) of water and microwave uncovered for 1 minute (at 800 watts), or until the water is absorbed; let cool.
- Medium dice the **cucumber**. Hull and slice the **strawberries**.
- Combine the **cucumber**, **strawberries**, **mint** leaves, and **oil** with the **couscous**. Add salt and pepper; serve.

SHRIMP AND MANGO SALAD

Mango
x 1

Arugula
1¾ ounces (50 g)

Shrimp
x 16 (cooked and peeled)

Shrimp chips
x 10

👤👤👤👤

🧂 **Salt, pepper**

🫗 **Drizzle of extra-virgin olive oil**

🕐
Preparation time: 10 min.

- Peel and dice the **mango**. In a serving dish, combine the **mango** with the **arugula** and **shrimp**. Add salt and pepper.
- Just before serving, crumble the **shrimp chips** and add them to the dish. Serve immediately with a drizzle of oil.

GOAT CHEESE–ZUCCHINI POCKETS

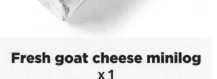

**Feuilles de brick
(or phyllo dough)
x 4 sheets**

**Zucchini
x 1**

**Fresh goat cheese minilog
x 1**

**Mint
4 sprigs**

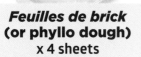

🧂 **Pepper**

**4 tbsp (60 mL)
vegetable oil**

**Preparation time: 5 min.
Cooking time: 35 min.**

- Preheat the oven to 400°F/210°C.
- Carefully brush each sheet of **dough** with 1 tbsp (15 mL) of **oil**. Thinly slice the **zucchini** into rounds and place them in the center of each **dough** sheet along with pieces of **goat cheese** and **mint** leaves. Sprinkle with pepper. Fold over the sides of the **dough** layers in toward the center to make pockets.
- Bake for 35 minutes, or until golden and crisp; serve immediately.

BAKED GOAT CHEESE-TOMATO TOASTS

Tomatoes
x 2

Fresh goat cheese minilog
x 1

Basil
16 leaves

White sandwich bread
4 slices

🧍🧍🧍🧍

🧂 **Salt, pepper**

🫗 **Drizzle of extra-virgin olive oil**

🕐

Preparation time: 5 min.
Cooking time: 15 min.

- Preheat the oven to 350°F/180°C.
- Slice the **tomatoes** and **cheese** into rounds of equal thickness and divide them and the **basil** leaves among the slices of **bread**. Add salt and pepper and a drizzle of oil over each and bake for 15 minutes, or until the **bread** is golden around the edges and the **cheese** is slightly melted; serve.

BAKED ASPARAGUS WITH PARMESAN-BUTTER CRUMB TOPPING

All-purpose flour
1 cup (3½ ounces/100 g)

Unsalted butter
7 tbsp (3½ ounces/100 g),
at room temperature

Parmesan cheese shavings
3½ ounces (100 g)

Asparagus
2 small bunches

👤👤👤👤

🧂 **Salt, pepper**

🕐

Preparation time: 10 min.
Cooking time: 25 min.

- Preheat the oven to 400°F/210°C.
- Knead together the **flour**, **butter**, and **Parmesan** to form a crumbly topping.
- Cut up the **asparagus** without peeling it, removing the tough stem ends. Divide the **asparagus** among 4 ramekins. Sprinkle the topping over the **asparagus**. Add salt and pepper and bake for 25 minutes, or until the topping is golden. Serve hot.

MUSSELS WITH GARLIC AND PARSLEY

Garlic
5 cloves

Flat-leaf parsley
½ bunch

Unsalted butter
10 tbsp (5¼ ounces/150 g),
at room temperature

Mussels
x 40 (large), cleaned,
beards removed

Preparation time: 10 min.
Cooking time: 8 min.

- Peel and chop the **garlic**. Chop the **parsley**. Combine the **butter** with the **garlic** and **parsley**. Cook the **mussels** in a pan for 5 minutes, or until they open. Let cool, then remove the shells (do not discard).
- Preheat the oven to 350°F/180°C.
- Place 2 **mussels** in each shell, spoon the garlic-parsley mixture over the top, and bake for 3 minutes, or until warmed. Serve immediately.

CLAMS WITH CILANTRO AND TOMATO

Cilantro
2 bunches

Unsalted butter
11 tbsp (5½ ounces/160 g),
at room temperature

Clams
x 48 (washed well)

Cherry tomatoes
x 15

🧍🧍🧍🧍

Preparation time: 10 min.
Cooking time: 8 min.

- Chop the **cilantro** and combine it with the **butter**.
- Cook the **clams** with ⅔ cup (150 mL) of water in a pot over low heat for 5 minutes, or until they open. Let cool, then remove the shells (do not discard).
- Preheat the oven to 350°F/180°C.
- Quarter the **tomatoes**. Place 2 **clams** in each shell, then top with the butter-cilantro mixture and a **tomato** wedge. Bake for 3 minutes, or until warmed. Serve immediately.

CREAM OF CELERY SOUP WITH PARMESAN

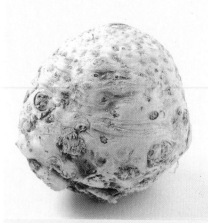

Celery root
1⅛ lb (500 g)

Potatoes
3½ ounces (100 g)

Heavy cream
1⅓ cups (330 mL)

Grated Parmesan cheese
3 ounces (80 g)

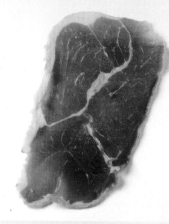

Prosciutto
4 slices

Rustic bread
4 slices

👤👤👤👤

🧂🧂 **Salt, pepper**

🫗 **Drizzle of extra-virgin olive oil**

🕐

Preparation time: 15 min.
Cooking time: 55 min.

- Peel and dice the **celery root** and **potatoes** and cook them in a pot over low heat with the **cream** and 3 cups (700 mL) of water for 45 minutes, or until tender.
- Remove from the heat and add three fourths of the **Parmesan**. Blend using an immersion blender until smooth.
- Preheat the oven to 350°F/180°C.
- Place 1 **prosciutto** slice on each slice of **bread**. Sprinkle with the remaining **Parmesan** and bake for 10 minutes.
- Ladle the soup into bowls and serve with a drizzle of oil and 1 slice of toast.

ORANGE-COCONUT SEAFOOD SOUP

Cherry tomatoes
x 16

Scallops (with coral)
x 8

Peas
7 ounces (200 g), fresh or frozen

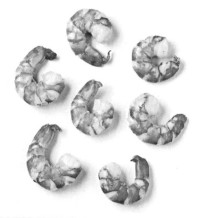

Shrimp
x 20 (cooked and peeled)

Orange juice
⅓ cup (100 mL)

Coconut milk
1 cup (250 mL)

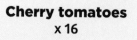 Salt, pepper

Preparation time: 5 min.
Cooking time: 8 min.

- Halve the **tomatoes**.
- Combine all the ingredients in a saucepan. Bring to a boil and let cook for 3 minutes, or until the **shrimp** and **scallops** are just cooked through and the vegetables are tender.
- Add salt and pepper; serve.

PEA AND PROSCIUTTO VELOUTÉ

Coconut milk
2 cups (500 mL)

Prosciutto
5 slices

Peas
1⅓ lb (600 g), fresh or frozen

👤👤👤👤

🧂🧂 **Salt, pepper**

⏱

Preparation time: 5 min.
Cooking time: 5 min.

• Pour the **coconut milk** into a saucepan. Add 4 slices of the **prosciutto** and all the **peas**. Bring to a boil and let cook for 30 seconds, then pour this mixture into a blender. Add salt and pepper and blend (in batches, if necessary, to prevent splattering).

• Serve immediately with torn pieces of the remaining slice of **prosciutto** scattered on top.

TOMATO, CANTALOUPE, AND STRAWBERRY GAZPACHO

Tomatoes
x 4

Fresh strawberries
x 10

Cantaloupe
x 1 (small)

Basil
1 small bunch

🧂🧂 **Salt, pepper**

Drizzle of extra-virgin olive oil

🕐 **Preparation time: 5 min.**

• Quarter the **tomatoes**. Hull the **strawberries**. Scoop out the seeds from the **cantaloupe**, peel, then medium dice the flesh.

• Place the **tomatoes**, **cantaloupe**, and **strawberries** in a blender and blend until smooth. Add salt and pepper, transfer to a bowl, and refrigerate until chilled.

• Divide the soup among bowls with a drizzle of oil and a **basil** leaf on top; serve.

ASPARAGUS MINESTRONE

Cherry tomatoes
x 20

Asparagus
1 bunch

Chicken bouillon
1 extra-large cube

Elbow macaroni
3½ ounces (100 g)

Peas
7 ounces (200 g), fresh or frozen

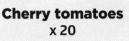 Salt, pepper

Drizzle of extra-virgin olive oil

Preparation time: 5 min.
Cooking time: 15 min.

- Halve the **tomatoes**.
- Cut up the **asparagus** (discard the tough stem ends) and place in a saucepan with the **tomatoes**, **bouillon**, **macaroni**, **peas**, and 4¼ cups (1 L) of water. Bring to a boil, reduce the heat to low, and let cook for 10 minutes, or until the vegetables are tender.
- Add salt and pepper and a drizzle of oil; serve hot.

CREAMY MUSHROOM SOUP WITH LARDONS

Bacon lardons
5¼ ounces (150 g)

White button mushrooms
1⅛ lb (500 g)

Chicken broth
Just over ¾ cup (200 mL)

Heavy cream
1⅓ cups (330 mL)

Soy sauce
4 tbsp (60 mL)

Cilantro
4 sprigs

👤👤👤👤

🧂 Pepper

🫗 Large drizzle of sunflower oil

🕐

Preparation time: 15 min.
Cooking time: 35 min.

- Sauté the **lardons** in a dry skillet until lightly browned.
- Slice the **mushrooms**. In a small pot, sauté the **mushrooms** with the oil for 5 minutes, then add the **broth**, **cream**, and **soy sauce**. Simmer for 30 minutes, add pepper, then blend using an immersion blender until smooth.
- Serve with the **lardons** and **cilantro** leaves on top.

SHRIMP AND WATERMELON SOUP

Oranges
x 3

**Mixed berry–flavored
green tea**
1½ cups (350 mL)

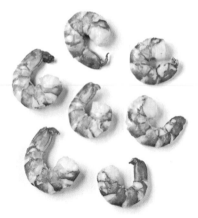

Shrimp
x 12 (cooked and peeled)

Watermelon wedge
7 ounces (200 g)

Mint
8 leaves

Salt, pepper

**Drizzle of extra-virgin
olive oil**

Preparation time: 10 min.

• Juice the **oranges**. Brew and chill the **tea**, then combine the juice with the **tea**. Chop the **shrimp**. Dice the flesh of the **watermelon**.

• Divide the **shrimp** and **watermelon** among 4 bowls and add the **mint** leaves. Pour the orange juice–tea mixture into the bowls, and add salt and pepper and a drizzle of oil; serve.

PEASANT SOUP

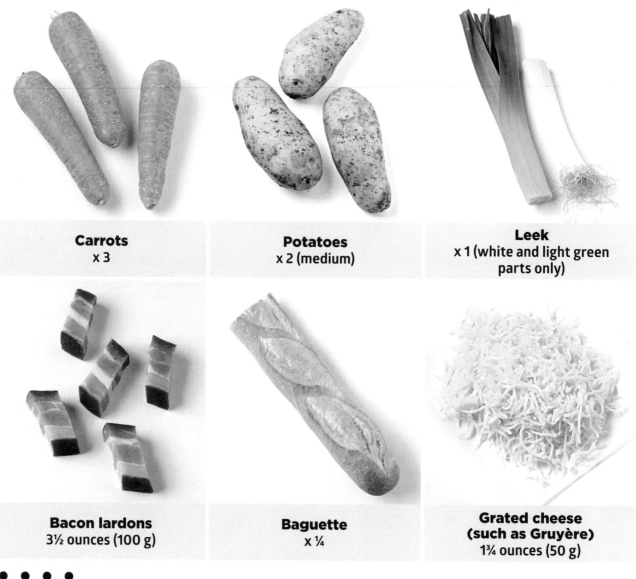

Carrots
x 3

Potatoes
x 2 (medium)

Leek
x 1 (white and light green
parts only)

Bacon lardons
3½ ounces (100 g)

Baguette
x ¼

**Grated cheese
(such as Gruyère)**
1¾ ounces (50 g)

👥👥👥👥

🧂🧂 **Salt, pepper**

🕐

**Preparation time: 15 min.
Cooking time: 60 min.**

- Cut off the root end of the leeks. Halve the leeks lengthwise, rinse, then cut them into thirds crosswise.
- Peel the **carrots** and **potatoes**. Thinly slice all the vegetables.
- Bring 6 cups (1.5 L) of water to a boil in a saucepan, add the vegetables and **lardons**, and cook over low heat for 45 minutes, or until the vegetables are tender.
- Preheat the broiler. Transfer the soup to an oven-safe soup terrine. Slice the **baguette**. Place the slices on top, then the grated **cheese**. Cook under the broiler for 10 minutes, or just until the cheese is melted and golden. Add salt and pepper to taste.

QUICK THAI SOUP

Turkey cutlets
x 3

Lemongrass
2 stalks

White button mushrooms
7 ounces (200 g), small

Coconut milk
2 cups (500 mL)

Serrano chile pepper
x 1 (small)

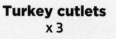

Salt, pepper

Preparation time: 5 min.
Cooking time: 5 min.
Resting time: 10 min.

- Cut the **turkey cutlets** into small pieces. Thinly slice the **lemongrass**.
- Place the **turkey** and **mushrooms** in a large microwave-safe bowl with the **lemongrass**, **coconut milk**, **chile**, and just over ¾ cup (200 mL) of water. Add salt and pepper, cover with plastic wrap, and microwave for 5 minutes (at 800 watts), or until the **turkey** is cooked through, stirring occasionally.
- Let cool for 10 minutes, then remove the plastic wrap and serve.

ASIAN CHICKEN NOODLE SOUP

Lemongrass
2 stalks

Chicken bouillon
3 extra-large cubes

Star anise
x 6

Chicken breasts
x 2

Spaghetti noodles
5¼ ounces (150 g)

Thai basil
2 bunches

4 to 6

Salt, pepper

Preparation time: 10 min.
Cooking time: 22 min.

- Thinly slice the **lemongrass**.
- In a saucepan over low heat, combine the **lemongrass**, **bouillon** cubes, **star anise**, and 2 quarts (2 L) of water. Cook for 12 minutes.
- Chop the **chicken**. Break the **noodles** in half. Add the **chicken** and **noodles** and cook for 10 more minutes, or until the chicken is cooked through. Remove from the heat, add **basil** leaves and salt and pepper, and serve immediately.

FOIE GRAS RAVIOLI AND CHERRY SOUP

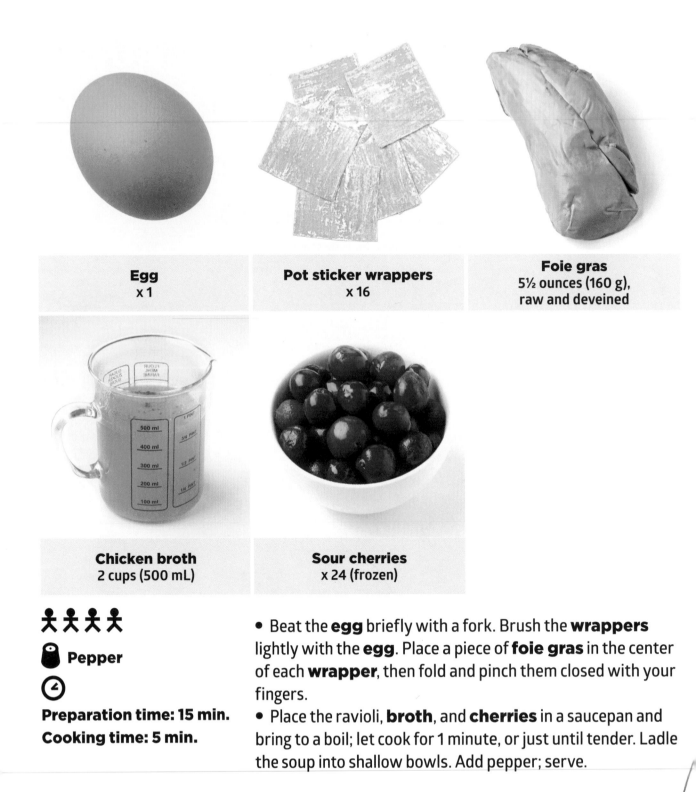

Egg
x 1

Pot sticker wrappers
x 16

Foie gras
5½ ounces (160 g),
raw and deveined

Chicken broth
2 cups (500 mL)

Sour cherries
x 24 (frozen)

👤👤👤👤

🧂 **Pepper**

🕐

Preparation time: 15 min.
Cooking time: 5 min.

• Beat the **egg** briefly with a fork. Brush the **wrappers** lightly with the **egg**. Place a piece of **foie gras** in the center of each **wrapper**, then fold and pinch them closed with your fingers.

• Place the ravioli, **broth**, and **cherries** in a saucepan and bring to a boil; let cook for 1 minute, or just until tender. Ladle the soup into shallow bowls. Add pepper; serve.

SALMON AND RAVIOLI SOUP

Cucumber
x ¼

Small cheese ravioli
9 ounces (250 g), frozen

Diced salmon
3⅛ ounces (90 g),
boneless and skinless

Chicken broth
2½ cups (600 mL)

👤👤👤👤

🧂 **Pepper**

⏱

Preparation time: 5 min.
Cooking time: 5 min.
Resting time: 2 min.

- Small dice the **cucumber**. Divide the **cucumber**, **ravioli**, and **salmon** among 4 bowls.
- Bring the **broth** to a boil, then pour it into the bowls. Add pepper, let sit for 2 minutes, and serve.

GOAT CHEESE AND BASIL RAVIOLI

Egg
x 1

Pot sticker wrappers
x 16

Goat cheese
x 3 small rounds

Basil
1 bunch

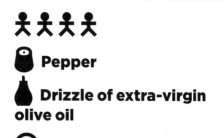

Pepper

Drizzle of extra-virgin olive oil

Preparation time: 15 min.
Cooking time: 7 min.

• Beat the **egg** briefly with a fork. Brush the **wrappers** lightly with the **egg**. Place a small piece of the **cheese** and 1 **basil** leaf in the center of each **wrapper**, then fold and pinch them closed with your fingers.
• Bring a saucepan of water to a boil and cook the ravioli for 2 minutes, or just until tender. Drain, add pepper, and serve immediately with the remaining **basil** and a drizzle of oil.

TUNA AND OLIVE PASTA SALAD

Farfalle pasta
9 ounces (250 g)

Mixed herbs (dill, chives, mint, parsley)
1 bunch

Tuna in oil
1 can (3½ ounces/100 g)

Olive tapenade
3 tbsp (45 mL)

Salt, pepper

Preparation time: 5 min.
Cooking time: 15 min.

- Cook the **pasta** in a saucepan of boiling salted water until al dente. Drain, then toss with a fork.
- Chop the **herbs**.
- Combine the **tuna** and the oil from the can with the **pasta**, then stir in the **herbs** and the **tapenade**. Add salt and pepper; serve.

ZUCCHINI AND PROSCIUTTO LASAGNA

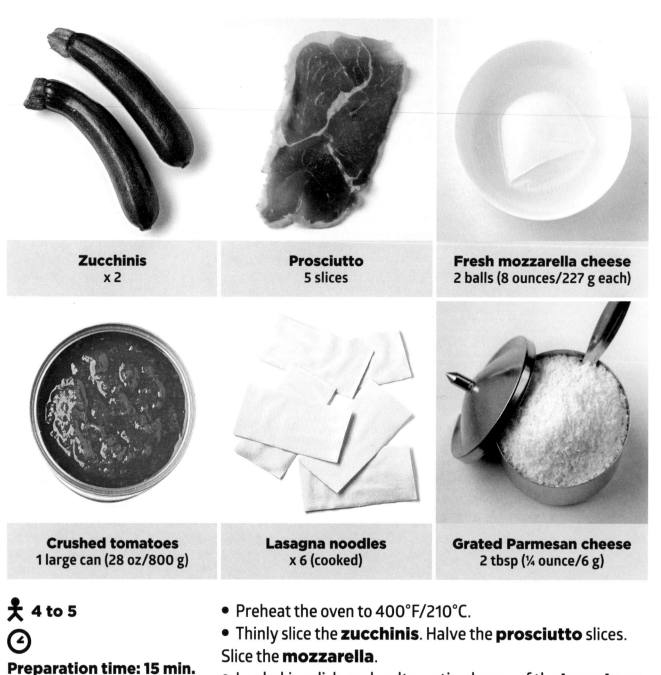

Zucchinis
x 2

Prosciutto
5 slices

Fresh mozzarella cheese
2 balls (8 ounces/227 g each)

Crushed tomatoes
1 large can (28 oz/800 g)

Lasagna noodles
x 6 (cooked)

Grated Parmesan cheese
2 tbsp (¼ ounce/6 g)

4 to 5

Preparation time: 15 min.
Cooking time: 45 min.

- Preheat the oven to 400°F/210°C.
- Thinly slice the **zucchinis**. Halve the **prosciutto** slices. Slice the **mozzarella**.
- In a baking dish, make alternating layers of the **tomatoes**, **zucchini**, **prosciutto**, **mozzarella**, and **noodles**. Sprinkle the **Parmesan** on top and bake for 45 minutes, or until the cheese is golden and the tomatoes are bubbling.

SPAGHETTI WITH PUTTANESCA SAUCE

Crushed tomatoes
1 large can (28 oz/800 g)

**Black olives
(Greek marinated)
x 20**

Capers
3 tbsp (1¼ ounces/36 g)

Anchovies in olive oil
1 can (about 14 fillets)

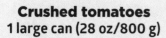

Spaghetti noodles
12 ounces (350 g)

**Preparation time: 10 min.
Cooking time: 10 min.**

• In a skillet over low heat, cook the **tomatoes** with the **olives**, **capers**, and **anchovies** (with the oil from the can) for 10 minutes, or until warmed through.
• Meanwhile, cook the **spaghetti** to al dente in a saucepan of boiling salted water.
• Drain, then add the **noodles** to the skillet and stir to coat; serve immediately.

SAUSAGE AND PENNE PASTA

Smoked sausage links
x 2

Crushed tomatoes
1 large can (28 oz/800 g)

Bouquets garnis
(bay leaf, thyme)
x 2

Garlic powder
1 tsp

Penne pasta
12 ounces (350 g)

👤👤👤👤

🧂🧂 Salt, pepper

🫗 1 tbsp (15 mL)
flavorless cooking oil

🕐

Preparation time: 10 min.
Cooking time: 16 min.

- Slice the **sausage** into rounds and cook them in a skillet with the oil for 1 minute. Add the **tomatoes**, **bouquets garnis**, and **garlic powder**. Simmer over low heat for 15 minutes, while stirring.
- Meanwhile, cook the **pasta** to al dente in boiling salted water; drain.
- Add the **pasta** to the skillet, stir to coat, then add salt and pepper; serve.

SPAGHETTI WITH SARDINES

Spaghetti noodles
12 ounces (350 g)

Organic limes
x 3

Toasted white bread
x 5 slices

Sardines in olive oil
2 cans (about 4 ounces/113 g each),
preferably with lemon

Baby spinach
3 handfuls

🧍🧍🧍🧍

🧂🧂 **Salt, pepper**

🕐

**Preparation time: 5 min.
Cooking time: 15 min.**

- Cook the **spaghetti** to al dente in a saucepan of boiling salted water.
- Meanwhile, zest and juice the **limes**, then crumble the **toast**.
- Drain the **pasta** (reserve some of the pasta water), then place the **pasta** in a skillet with 1 tbsp (15 mL) of the pasta water, the **sardines** (with their oil), **toast**, and **lime** zest and juice. Add salt and pepper and cook for 5 minutes, while stirring.
- Add the **spinach** off the heat, toss gently to combine, and serve.

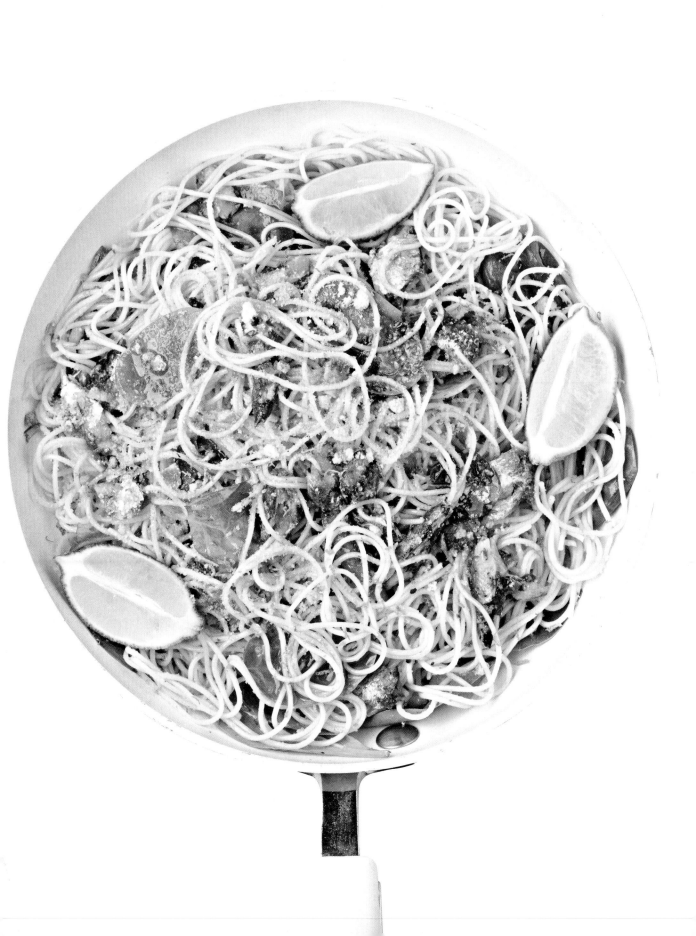

QUICK PENNE ARRABBIATA

Eggplants
x 2 (small)

Chorizo
x ½ link (about 4 ounces/113 g)

Tomatoes
x 2

Crushed tomatoes
1 small can (14 ounces/400 g)

Penne pasta
12 ounces (350 g)

Grated Parmesan cheese
4 tbsp (½ ounce/12 g)

Preparation time: 5 min.
Cooking time: 15 min.

- Medium dice the **eggplants**. Slice the **chorizo** and chop the **tomatoes**.
- Add the **eggplant**, **chorizo**, chopped and crushed **tomatoes**, and **pasta** to a large microwave-safe bowl with ⅔ cup (150 mL) of water. Cover with plastic wrap and microwave for 15 minutes (at 800 watts), or until the **pasta** is just al dente, stirring occasionally. Sprinkle with the **Parmesan**; serve.

SCALLOP TAGLIATELLE

Scallops
8 pieces (without coral)

***Jamón pata negra* or other
Spanish salt-cured ham**
4 slices

Asparagus
x 12 stalks

Fresh tagliatelle pasta
14 ounces (400 g)

Extra-virgin olive oil
4 tbsp (60 mL)

Heavy cream
⅓ cup (100 mL)

**Preparation time: 15 min.
Cooking time: 15 min.**

- Halve the **scallops** and cut the **ham** into thin strips. Halve the **asparagus** lengthwise and chop the tips (discard the tough stem ends).
- Cook the **pasta** to al dente in boiling salted water; drain.
- In a skillet, cook the **asparagus** in the **oil** for 5 minutes, or until slightly softened. Add the **scallops** and cook for 1 minute, then add the cooked **pasta**, **ham**, and **cream**. Cook for 1 more minute, or just until the **scallops** are cooked through. Stir to combine; serve.

CHEESY TUNA PASTA CASSEROLE

Fusilli pasta
12 ounces (350 g)

Roasted red peppers
9 ounces (250 g), drained

Fresh mozzarella cheese
2 balls (8 ounces/227 g each)

Dried oregano
1 tbsp

Tuna in oil
1 can (3½ ounces/100 g)

Grated Cheddar cheese
1½ ounces (40 g)

Preparation time: 10 min.
Cooking time: 35 min.

- Preheat the oven to 400°F/210°C.
- Cook the **pasta** to al dente in a saucepan of boiling salted water; drain.
- Chop the **red peppers**. Slice the **mozzarella**.
- Transfer the **pasta**, **red peppers**, **oregano**, **tuna** (with the oil from the can), and **mozzarella** to a baking dish and stir to combine. Top with the **Cheddar** and bake for 25 minutes, or until the cheese is melted and golden.

BAKED GNOCCHI ARRABBIATA

Gnocchi
2 packages (16 ounces/454 g each)

Chorizo
8 slices

Crushed tomatoes
1 small can (14 ounces/400 g)

Grated Parmesan cheese
4 tbsp (½ ounce/12 g)

👤👤👤👤

🧂 **Pepper**

🕑
Preparation time: 5 min.
Cooking time: 15 min.

• Preheat the oven to 400°F/210°C.
• Place the **gnocchi**, **chorizo**, and **tomatoes** in a baking dish. Sprinkle with the **Parmesan** and bake for 15 minutes, or just until the **gnocchi** are tender. Add pepper and serve.

SCALLOP AND SAFFRON PENNE

Penne pasta
12 ounces (350 g)

Scallops (with coral)
x 12

Heavy cream
1⅓ cups (330 mL)

Saffron
10 threads (or 1 small pinch)

Basil
1 bunch

Salt, pepper

1 tbsp (15 mL)
flavorless cooking oil
Preparation time: 10 min.
Cooking time: 14 min.

• Cook the **pasta** to al dente in a saucepan of boiling salted water; drain.
• In a skillet, cook the **scallops** in the oil for 1 minute, or until lightly browned. Add the **cream**, **saffron**, and **basil** leaves and cook for 2 more minutes over low heat, or just until the **scallops** are cooked through.
• Add the **pasta** to the skillet. Add salt and pepper and stir to coat; serve.

SQUID-INK PAELLA

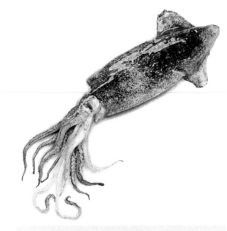

Squid
1⅛ lb (500 g), cleaned

Paella rice (short grain)
14 ounces (400 g)

Chicken broth
4¼ cups (1 L)

Dried oregano
1 tbsp

Squid ink
3 packets (or 3 tbsp/
90 mL from a jar)

Extra-virgin olive oil
4 tbsp (60 mL)

👤👤👤👤

🕐

Preparation time: 5 min.
Cooking time: 45 min.

- Preheat the oven to 350°F/180°C.
- Chop the **squid** into large pieces. In a large baking dish, place the **squid**, **rice**, **broth**, **oregano**, and **squid ink**. Add the **oil**, then evenly spread the mixture out in the dish. Bake for 45 minutes, or just until the **squid** pieces are cooked through.
- Serve from the baking dish.

ASPARAGUS RISOTTO

Asparagus
1 bunch

Arborio rice (for risotto)
10½ ounces (300 g)

Chicken broth
2 cups (500 mL)

White wine
1¼ cups (300 mL)

Grated Parmesan cheese
1¾ ounces (50 g)

👤👤👤👤

🧂 Pepper

🕐
Preparation time: 5 min.
Cooking time: 20 min.

• Cut the **asparagus** into pieces (do not peel them; discard the tough stem ends). Place the **asparagus**, **rice**, **broth**, and **wine** in a pot over low heat. Cook for 20 minutes, stirring, or until the **rice** is tender and the liquid is almost absorbed.

• Add the **Parmesan** and pepper, and stir to combine; serve immediately.

CHICKEN PAELLA

Chorizo
x ½ link (about 4 ounces/113 g)

Red bell pepper
x 1

Paella rice (short grain)
14 ounces (400 g)

Chicken legs
x 2 (halved at the joint)

Saffron threads
2 small pinches

Mussels
x 30 (cleaned, beards removed)

Pepper

Preparation time: 5 min.
Cooking time: 45 min.

- Preheat the oven to 350°F/180°C.
- Slice the **chorizo**. Remove the stem and seed the **bell pepper**; thinly slice the flesh.
- Place the **chorizo**, **bell pepper**, **rice**, **chicken** pieces, and **saffron** in a baking dish with 4¼ cups (1 L) of water. Add pepper and combine. Bake for 35 minutes.
- Add the **mussels**, stir to combine, then cook for 10 more minutes, or until golden on top and the **chicken** is cooked through; serve immediately.

SCALLOP RISOTTO

Arborio rice (for risotto)
10½ ounces (300 g)

Chicken broth
2 cups (500 mL)

Saffron threads
2 small pinches

White wine
1¼ cups (300 mL)

Scallops (with coral)
1¾ lb (800 g)

👥👥 Salt, pepper

⏱

Preparation time: 5 min.
Cooking time: 20 min.

- Place the **rice**, **broth**, **saffron**, and **wine** in a pot. Cook over low heat for 15 minutes, stirring.
- Add the **scallops** and cook for 5 more minutes, stirring, or just until the **rice** is tender, the liquid almost absorbed, and the **scallops** cooked through. Add salt and pepper; serve.

ZUCCHINI AND GOAT CHEESE TART

Zucchinis
x 2

Goat cheese
x 2 small rounds

Egg
x 1

Dried oregano
1 tbsp

Pie crust dough
x 1 sheet (8 ounces/227 g)

👤👤👤👤

🧂🧂 **Salt, pepper**

🕐

Preparation time: 10 min.
Cooking time: 45 min.

- Preheat the oven to 350°F/180°C.
- Cut off the stem ends of the **zucchinis**. Grate the **zucchinis**. Cut up the **cheese**.
- In a large bowl, lightly beat the **egg** with a fork. Add the **zucchini**, **cheese**, and **oregano** to the bowl. Add salt and pepper.
- Unroll the **dough** sheet onto an 8-inch (20-cm) parchment-lined tart pan and fold any excess dough over onto the inside. Pour the filling into the pan and bake for 45 minutes, or until golden on top.

HAMBURGER PIZZA

Pizza dough
x 1 (about 12 ounces/340 g),
fresh or frozen

Canned crushed tomatoes
4 tbsp

Ground beef
4½ ounces (125 g)

Bacon
3 thin slices

Grated Cheddar cheese
1 handful (about 2⅛ ounces/60 g)

🧍🧍🧍🧍

🫙 **Drizzle of extra-virgin olive oil**

🕐

Preparation time: 5 min.
Cooking time: 25 min.

- Preheat the oven to 400°F/210°C.
- Roll out the **dough** onto a parchment-lined baking sheet. Spread the **tomatoes** on top to about 1 inch (3 cm) from the edge. Roll the **ground beef** into small meatballs and distribute them on top. Add the strips of **bacon**, then the **Cheddar**. Fold in the edges of the **dough** to make a border and bake for 25 minutes, or until the meatballs are cooked through and the edges of the crust are golden.
- Serve, drizzled with oil.

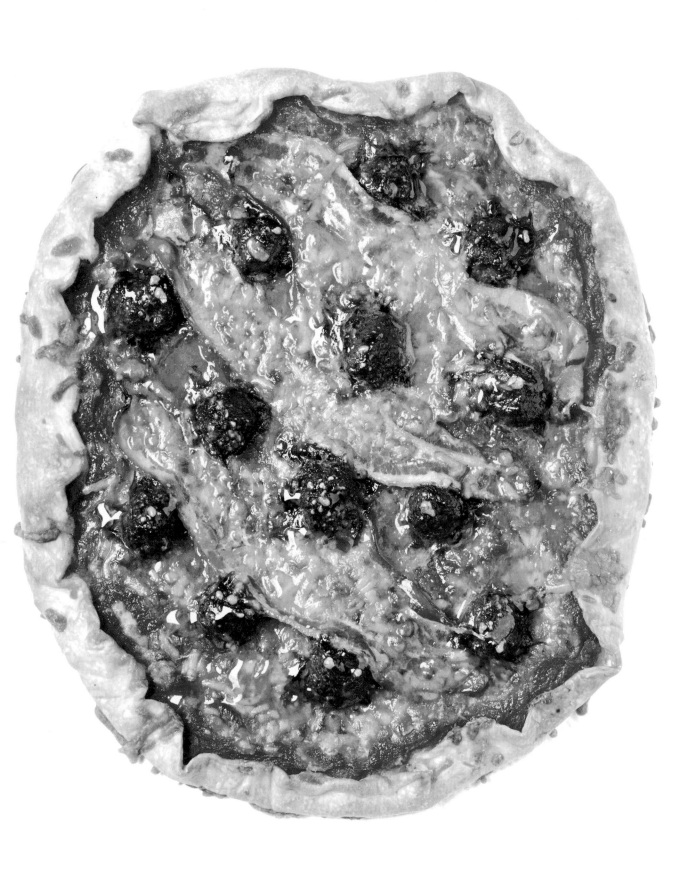

SAUSAGE AND PARMESAN PIZZA

Red onions
x 4

Chipolatas or other fresh sausages
x 4

Pizza dough
x 1 (about 12 ounces/340 g), fresh or frozen

Grated Parmesan cheese
4 tbsp (½ ounce/12 g)

👤👤👤👤

🍐 **2 tbsp (30 mL) flavorless cooking oil**
Drizzle of extra-virgin olive oil

🕐

Preparation time: 10 min.
Cooking time: 50 min.

- Preheat the oven to 400°F/210°C.
- Finely chop the **onions** and slice the **sausages**. In a saucepan with the flavorless oil, cook the **onions** and the **sausages** for 25 minutes, or until softened and browned.
- Roll out the **dough** onto a parchment-lined baking sheet. Spread the cooked topping over the **dough** to about 1 inch (3 cm) from the edge, then sprinkle with the **Parmesan**. Bake for 25 minutes, or until golden and the **sausages** are cooked through; serve with a drizzle of olive oil.

PEAR, CHORIZO, AND PARMESAN PIZZA

Pizza dough
x 1 (about 12 ounces/340 g),
fresh or frozen

Pear
x 1

Chorizo
10 slices

Parmesan cheese shavings
1¾ ounces (50 g)

👤👤👤👤

🧂 Pepper

🫗 Drizzle of extra-virgin olive oil

🕐
Preparation time: 10 min.
Cooking time: 25 min.

- Preheat the oven to 400°F/210°C.
- Roll out the **dough** onto a parchment-lined baking sheet. Peel and thinly slice the **pear**. Halve the **chorizo** slices. Distribute the **pear** and **chorizo** on top of the **dough** in an overlapping pattern to about 1 inch (3 cm) from the edge.
- Crumble the **Parmesan** on top and bake for 25 minutes, or until golden. Add pepper and serve, drizzled with oil.

VEGETABLE PIZZA

Pizza dough
x 1 (about 12 ounces/340 g),
fresh or frozen

Zucchinis
x 2

White button mushrooms
x 10

Red bell pepper
x 1

Dried oregano
1 tbsp

**Grated cheese
(such as Gruyère)**
2⅛ ounces (60 g)

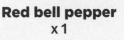

Salt, pepper

**Preparation time: 5 min.
Cooking time: 25 min.**

- Preheat the oven to 350°F/180°C.
- Roll out the **dough** onto a parchment-lined baking sheet. Slice the **zucchinis** and **mushrooms**. Remove the stem and seed the **bell pepper**; cut the flesh into strips.
- In a large bowl, combine the **oregano** and vegetables. Add salt and pepper, stir, then spread this mixture over the **dough** to about 1 inch (3 cm) from the edge. Sprinkle with the **cheese** and bake for 25 minutes, or until golden.

APPLE AND CHEESE PIZZA

Pizza dough
x 1 (about 12 ounces/340 g),
fresh or frozen

Apple
x 1

Reblochon cheese (or other soft Alpine cheese)
x ½ small round

Prosciutto
2 slices

👤👤👤👤

🌶 Pepper

🕐
**Preparation time: 10 min.
Cooking time: 25 min.**

- Preheat the oven to 400°F/210°C.
- Roll out the **dough** onto a parchment-lined baking sheet. Peel, core, and slice the **apple** into thin wedges. Chop the **cheese** and **prosciutto**.
- Distribute the **apple**, **cheese**, and **prosciutto** on top of the **dough** to about 1 inch (3 cm) from the edge. Fold in the edges of the **dough** and bake for 25 minutes, or until golden. Add pepper. Serve hot.

WINTER SQUASH AND MEATBALL FLATBREAD

Pizza dough
x 1 (about 12 ounces/340 g),
fresh or frozen

Winter squash
14 ounces (400 g)

Ground sausage
9 ounces (250 g)

Grated Parmesan cheese
1¾ ounces (50 g)

Dried oregano
1 tbsp

Drizzle of extra-virgin olive oil

Preparation time: 10 min.
Cooking time: 25 min.

- Preheat the oven to 400°F/210°C.
- Roll out the **dough** onto a parchment-lined baking sheet. Peel and seed the **squash**; small dice the flesh. Roll the **sausage** into meatballs.
- Distribute the **squash** and meatballs on top of the dough to about 1 inch (3 cm) from the edge. Sprinkle with the **Parmesan** and **oregano**. Bake for 25 minutes, or until golden. Serve, drizzled with oil.

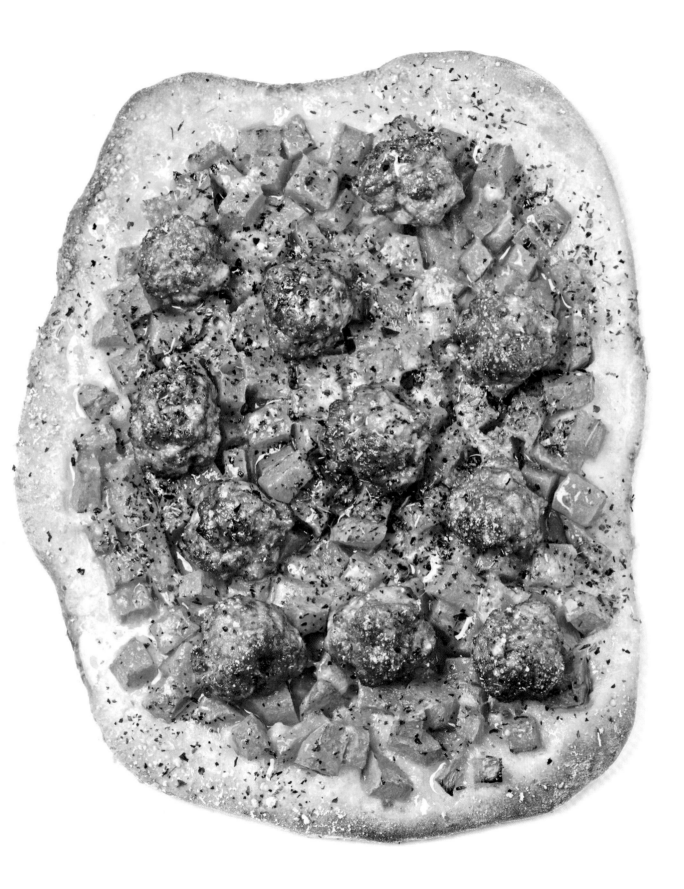

HAWAIIAN PIZZA

Pizza dough
x 1 (about 12 ounces/340 g), fresh or frozen

Pineapple
x ½

Chorizo
6 slices

Canned crushed tomatoes
5 tbsp

Grated Parmesan cheese
2 tbsp (¼ oz/6 g)

Drizzle of extra-virgin olive oil

Preparation time: 15 min.
Cooking time: 25 min.

- Preheat the oven to 400°F/210°C.
- Roll out the **dough** onto a parchment-lined baking sheet. Peel the **pineapple** and cut it into small pieces. Quarter the **chorizo** slices.
- Spread the **tomatoes** on the **dough** to about 1 inch (3 cm) from the edge, then distribute the **pineapple** and **chorizo** on top. Sprinkle with the **Parmesan** and bake for 25 minutes, or until golden. Serve, drizzled with oil.

FRESH TOMATO AND BASIL PIZZA

Pizza dough
x 1 (about 12 ounces/340 g),
fresh or frozen

Cherry tomatoes
x 40

Fresh mozzarella cheese
2 balls (8 ounces/227 g each)

Basil
1 bunch

♟♟♟♟

🧂 **Salt, pepper**

🫗 **Drizzle of extra-virgin olive oil**

🕐

Preparation time: 10 min.
Cooking time: 25 min.

- Preheat the oven to 400°F/210°C.
- Roll out the **dough** onto a parchment-lined baking sheet. Fold in the edge of the **dough** to form a border. Quarter the **tomatoes**. Slice the **mozzarella** and distribute it on top of the **dough**. Bake for 25 minutes, or until the **cheese** is melted and slightly browned. Remove from the oven.
- Cover the **cheese** with the **tomatoes** and **basil** leaves. Add salt and pepper and serve, drizzled with oil.

SAUERKRAUT AND KIELBASA FLATBREAD

Pie crust dough
x 1 sheet (8 ounces/227 g)

Kielbasa
x 4

Crème fraîche
2 tbsp (30 mL)

Cooked sauerkraut
3½ ounces (100 g)

Cumin Gouda cheese
1¾ ounces (50 g)

Preparation time: 5 min.
Cooking time: 25 min.

- Preheat the oven to 400°F/210°C.
- Unroll the **dough** sheet onto a parchment-lined baking sheet. Halve the **kielbasa** lengthwise.
- Spread the **crème fraîche** on top of the **dough** to about 1 inch (3 cm) from the edge. Add the **sauerkraut**, then the **kielbasa**. Grate the **Gouda** on top and bake for 25 minutes, or until golden; serve.

HAM AND SPINACH PIZZA WITH MUSTARD

Pizza dough
x 1 (about 12 ounces/340 g),
fresh or frozen

Mustard
3 tbsp (45 mL)

Greek yogurt
x 1 small container
(6 ounces/170 g)

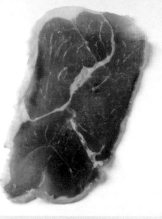

Prosciutto
5 slices

Baby spinach
1 oz (30 g)

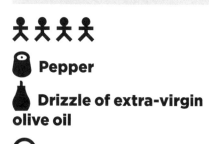

Pepper

Drizzle of extra-virgin olive oil

Preparation time: 5 min.
Cooking time: 25 min.

- Preheat the oven to 400°F/210°C.
- Roll out the **dough** onto a parchment-lined baking sheet. Combine the **mustard** and **yogurt** and spread it over the dough to about 1 inch (3 cm) from the edge. Place the **prosciutto** slices on top and bake for 25 minutes, or until the **prosciutto** is cooked and the edges of the **dough** are golden.
- Remove from the oven and add the **spinach** on top. Add pepper, drizzle with oil, and serve.

BELL PEPPER, MOZZARELLA, AND TUNA POCKET

Pizza dough
x 1 (about 12 ounces/340 g),
fresh or frozen

Red bell pepper
x 1

Fresh mozzarella cheese
1 ball (8 ounces/227 g)

Tuna in oil
1 can (3½ ounces/100 g)

Dried thyme
1 tbsp

Makes 1 pocket

◔

Preparation time: 5 min.
Cooking time: 15 min.

- Preheat the oven to 400°F/210°C.
- Roll out the **dough** onto a parchment-lined baking sheet. Remove the stem and seed the **bell pepper**; cut the flesh into strips. Slice the **mozzarella**.
- Distribute the **mozzarella**, **bell pepper**, **tuna** (reserve the oil), and **thyme** on top of the **dough** toward the center. Fold the edges in toward the center to form a pocket and bake for 15 minutes, or until golden.
- Serve with a drizzle of oil from the **tuna** can.

POTATO AND ZUCCHINI GRATIN

Zucchinis
x 2

Potatoes
x 2 (large)

Heavy cream
1⅓ cups (330 mL)

**Grated cheese
(such as Gruyère)**
1¾ ounces (50 g)

Salt, pepper

**Preparation time: 5 min.
Cooking time: 45 min.**

• Preheat the oven to 400°F/210°C.
• Thinly slice the **zucchinis** and **potatoes**. In a large bowl, combine them with the **cream** and **cheese**. Add salt and pepper.
• Arrange the vegetables in a baking dish and bake for 45 minutes, or until golden on top and the **cheese** is melted; serve.

TOMATOES STUFFED WITH GOAT CHEESE AND PROSCIUTTO

Goat cheese
x 2 small rounds

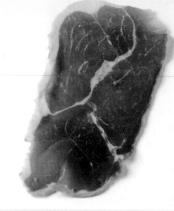

Prosciutto
2 slices

Tomatoes
x 4

👤👤👤👤

🧂 **Pepper**

🫗 **Drizzle of extra-virgin olive oil**

🕐

Preparation time: 5 min.
Cooking time: 20 min.

- Preheat the oven to 400°F/210°C.
- Halve the **cheese** and **prosciutto**. Cut the tops off the **tomatoes**, scoop out the flesh, and fill the **tomatoes** each with a piece of **prosciutto** and **cheese**.
- Replace the tops and bake for 20 minutes, or until the **cheese** is slightly melted and the **tomatoes** are softened. Add pepper. Serve, drizzled with oil.

148

BAKED CHORIZO AND MOZZARELLA EGGPLANTS

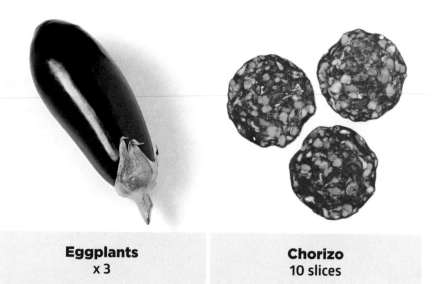

Eggplants
x 3

Chorizo
10 slices

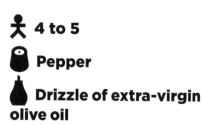

Fresh mozzarella cheese
3 balls (8 ounces/227 g each)

4 to 5

Pepper

Drizzle of extra-virgin olive oil

Preparation time: 5 min.
Cooking time: 45 min.

- Preheat the oven to 350°F/180°C.
- Halve the **eggplants** and **chorizo** slices. Slice the **mozzarella** into 6 slices per ball.
- Arrange the **eggplant** in a baking dish. On top of each half, overlap 3 pieces of **mozzarella** and 4 to 5 pieces of **chorizo**. Add pepper, drizzle with just over ¾ cup (200 mL) of water, and bake for 45 minutes, or until golden and the **cheese** is melted.
- Serve, drizzled with oil.

PARMESAN SWEET POTATO FRIES

Sweet potato
x 1 (large) or 2 (small)

Grated Parmesan cheese
1¾ ounces (50 g)

Salt, pepper

Drizzle of flavorless cooking oil

Preparation time: 10 min.
Cooking time: 10 min.

• Preheat the oven to 350°F/180°C.
• Peel and cut the **sweet potatoes** into sticks. Place them on a parchment-lined baking sheet. Add salt and pepper. Sprinkle with the **Parmesan** and drizzle with oil. Bake for 10 minutes, or until the **potatoes** are tender and the **Parmesan** is crisp and golden.
• Let cool, then serve with the crisped pieces of **Parmesan**.

BELL PEPPERS STUFFED WITH FETA AND TOMATO

Green bell peppers
x 4

Tomatoes
x 4

Feta cheese
2 packages (7 ounces/200 g each)

Herbes de Provence
4 tbsp

Drizzle of extra-virgin olive oil

Preparation time: 5 min.
Cooking time: 45 min.

- Preheat the oven to 400°F/210°C.
- Halve the **bell peppers** lengthwise and remove the seeds. Chop the **tomatoes**. Crumble the **feta**.
- Combine the **tomatoes**, **feta**, and **herbes de Provence** in a bowl. Spoon this mixture into the **peppers**. Drizzle oil over the top and bake for 45 minutes, or until the edges are browned and the **cheese** is melted; serve.

BACON-WRAPPED POTATO WEDGES

| **Potatoes**
x 12 (medium) | **Bacon**
16 thin slices |

Pepper

Preparation time: 15 min.
Cooking time: 25 min.

- Preheat the oven to 350°F/180°C.
- Cut the **potatoes** into thick wedges, and wrap each wedge with a small piece of **bacon**.
- Place them on a parchment-lined baking sheet, add pepper, and bake for 25 minutes, or until the **potatoes** are tender and the **bacon** crisp; serve.

MEDITERRANEAN-STYLE STUFFED CHILE PEPPERS

Preserved lemons
x 2

Ground sausage
9 ounces (250 g)

Couscous
2 tbsp (1 oz/25 g)

Whole green chile peppers
x 6

Crushed tomatoes
1 small can (14 ounces/400 g)

Salt, pepper

Preparation time: 10 min.
Cooking time: 25 min.

- Preheat the oven to 400°F/210°C.
- Small dice the **lemons** and combine them with the **sausage** and **couscous**. Halve the **chiles** lengthwise, remove the seeds, and stuff them with the sausage mixture.
- Pour the **tomatoes** into a baking dish and place the **chiles** on top. Add salt and pepper and bake for 25 minutes, or until lightly browned and the **sausage** is cooked through; serve.

ZUCCHINI AND FENNEL SAUTÉ

Zucchinis
x 2

Fennel
1 bulb

Fresh goat cheese minilog
x 1

Prosciutto
2 slices

👤👤👤👤

🧂 **Pepper**

🫗 **1 tbsp (15 mL) flavorless cooking oil**

🕐

Preparation time: 5 min.
Cooking time: 25 min.

• Thinly slice the **zucchinis** and finely chop the **fennel** bulb. Slice the **cheese** into 4 pieces. Halve the **prosciutto**.
• Brown the **zucchini** and **fennel** in a skillet with the oil, stirring occasionally, until softened and lightly browned. Add the **prosciutto** and **cheese** and cook over low heat for 10 minutes, or until the **prosciutto** is cooked through and the **cheese** slightly melted. Add pepper and serve.

ENDIVE AND CHORIZO GRATIN

Belgian endives
x 5

Chorizo
10 thin slices

Heavy cream
Just over ¾ cup (200 mL)

**Grated cheese
(such as Gruyère)**
1¾ ounces (50 g)

4 to 5

Pepper

Preparation time: 5 min.
Cooking time: 30 min.

- Preheat the oven to 400°F/210°C.
- Halve the **endives** lengthwise. Place a piece of **chorizo** on top of each half and place them in a baking dish.
- Combine the **cream** and **cheese**. Pour this mixture over the top of the **endives**, then add pepper.
- Bake for 30 minutes, or until the **endives** are browned and the **cheese** is melted; serve from the baking dish.

BAKED ITALIAN-STYLE TOMATOES

Roma tomatoes
x 8

Fresh mozzarella cheese
2 balls (8 ounces/227 g each)

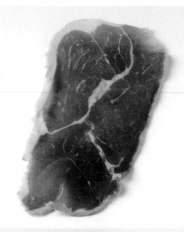

Prosciutto
4 slices

Basil
1 small bunch (24 large leaves)

Salt, pepper

Drizzle of extra-virgin olive oil

**Preparation time: 15 min.
Cooking time: 20 min.**

- Preheat the oven to 325°F/170°C.
- Make 3 deep incisions in each **tomato** (do not cut all the way through). Slice the **mozzarella** and tear the **prosciutto** into 24 small pieces. Into each incision, insert 1 slice of **mozzarella**, 1 piece of **prosciutto**, and 1 **basil** leaf.
- Place the **tomatoes** in a baking dish, add salt and pepper, and bake for 20 minutes, or until lightly browned and the **cheese** is melted. Serve hot, drizzled with oil.

MOUSSAKA

Eggplants
x 2

Ground beef
14 ounces (400 g)

Crushed tomatoes
1 small can (14 ounces/400 g)

**Grated cheese
(such as Gruyère)**
1¾ ounces (50 g)

Heavy cream
⅓ cup (100 mL)

👤👤👤👤

🧂🧂 Salt, pepper

🕐

**Preparation time: 5 min.
Cooking time: 1 hr.**

- Preheat the oven to 350°F/180°C.
- Thinly slice the **eggplants** and arrange them in a baking dish with the **ground beef**, **tomatoes**, **cheese**, and **cream**.
- Add salt and pepper and bake for 1 hour, or until golden on top. Serve immediately.

CAULIFLOWER IN A PASTRY CRUST

Cauliflower
x 1 (medium)

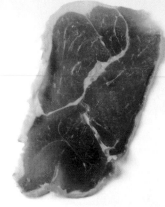

Prosciutto
4 slices

Cheddar cheese
6 slices

Dried thyme
2 tbsp

Pizza dough
x 1 (about 12 ounces/
340 g), fresh or frozen

👤👤👤👤

🧂🧂 Salt, pepper

🕐

Preparation time: 15 min.
Cooking time: 1 hr.

- Cook the whole **cauliflower** for 20 minutes in a saucepan of boiling salted water. Let cool.
- Preheat the oven to 350°F/180°C.
- Slice the **prosciutto** and **cheese** into small pieces. Make deep incisions in the **cauliflower** and insert the **prosciutto** and **Cheddar**. Sprinkle with the **thyme**. Add salt and pepper.
- Roll out the **dough** onto a parchment-lined baking sheet. Wrap the **cauliflower** in the **dough** and pinch it closed to seal it completely. Bake for 40 minutes, or until golden. Serve hot, sliced in wedges.

EGG AND MEATBALL RATATOUILLE

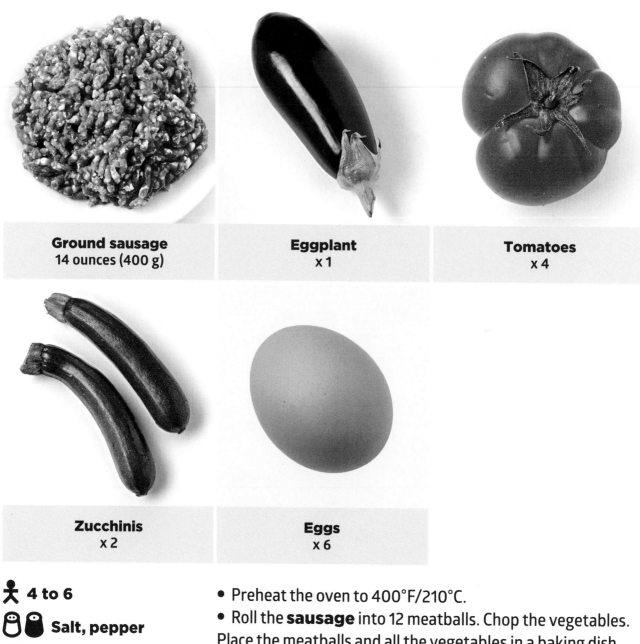

Ground sausage
14 ounces (400 g)

Eggplant
x 1

Tomatoes
x 4

Zucchinis
x 2

Eggs
x 6

🧍 4 to 6

🧂🧂 Salt, pepper

🕐

Preparation time: 10 min.
Cooking time: 40 min.

- Preheat the oven to 400°F/210°C.
- Roll the **sausage** into 12 meatballs. Chop the vegetables. Place the meatballs and all the vegetables in a baking dish. Add salt and pepper and bake for 35 minutes, or until lightly browned.
- Crack the **eggs** on top and bake for 5 more minutes, or until the **eggs** are cooked. Serve hot.

BAKED COPPA HAM POTATOES

Potatoes
x 2 (large)

Rosemary
2 sprigs

Coppa ham (or prosciutto)
8 thin slices (3½ ounces/100 g)

Grated Parmesan cheese
1 oz (30 g)

Preparation time: 5 min.
Cooking time: 35 min.

- Preheat the oven to 350°F/180°C.
- Boil the **potatoes**, skin on, for 10 minutes.
- Strip the **rosemary** leaves from the stems. Halve the **potatoes** lengthwise, place them in a baking dish, then place the **ham** and **rosemary** leaves on top of each.
- Sprinkle with the **Parmesan** and bake for 25 minutes, or until the ham is cooked through and the tops are golden. Serve very hot.

BAKED VEGETABLES PROVENÇAL

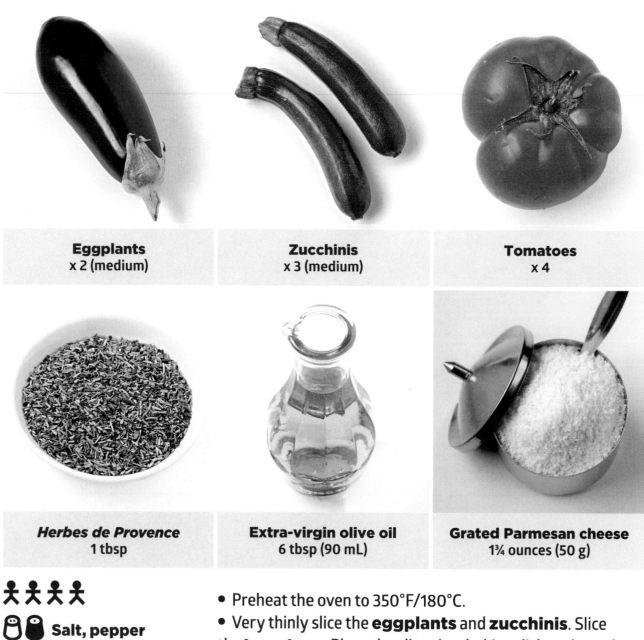

Eggplants
x 2 (medium)

Zucchinis
x 3 (medium)

Tomatoes
x 4

Herbes de Provence
1 tbsp

Extra-virgin olive oil
6 tbsp (90 mL)

Grated Parmesan cheese
1¾ ounces (50 g)

🧂 Salt, pepper

🕐

Preparation time: 10 min.
Cooking time: 50 min.

- Preheat the oven to 350°F/180°C.
- Very thinly slice the **eggplants** and **zucchinis**. Slice the **tomatoes**. Place the slices in a baking dish and evenly distribute the **herbes de Provence** and the **oil** over the top, then sprinkle on the **Parmesan**.
- Add salt and pepper and bake for 50 minutes, or until golden and bubbling.

MICROWAVE SCALLOPED POTATOES

Potatoes
x 3 (large)

Garlic
1 clove

Heavy cream
2 cups (500 mL)

**Grated cheese
(such as Gruyère)**
2 handfuls (about 3½ ounces/100 g)

Grated nutmeg
2 pinches

👤👤👤👤

🧂🧂 **Salt, pepper**

⏲

Preparation time: 5 min.
Cooking time: 25 min.

• Peel and very thinly slice the **potatoes**. Peel and chop the **garlic**.

• Combine the **potatoes** and **garlic** in a microwave-safe dish with the **cream**, half the **cheese**, and the **nutmeg**. Add salt and pepper.

• Sprinkle the remaining **cheese** on top and microwave uncovered for 25 minutes (at 800 watts), or until the **potatoes** are tender and the **cheese** is melted and golden; serve.

SCALLOPED HAM AND LEEKS

Leeks
x 4 (medium), white and light green parts only

Pressed ham
4 slices (outer rind removed), chopped

**Grated cheese
(such as Gruyère)**
3½ ounces (100 g)

Heavy cream
1⅔ cups (400 mL)

4 to 6

Salt, pepper

**Preparation time: 5 min.
Cooking time: 1 hr.**

- Preheat the oven to 350°F/180°C.
- Cut off the root end of the **leeks**. Halve the **leeks** lengthwise, rinse, then cut them into thirds crosswise.
- Combine the **leeks**, **ham**, **cheese**, and **cream** in a baking dish. Add salt and pepper. Bake for 1 hour, or until browned on top; serve very hot.

CHORIZO PIPÉRADE

Assorted bell peppers
x 4

Garlic
4 cloves

Vidalia or other sweet onions
x 2

Chorizo
x 1 link (about 8 ounces/227 g)

Extra-virgin olive oil
4 tbsp (60 mL)

🧍🧍🧍🧍

🧂🧂 Salt, pepper

🕑

Preparation time: 10 min.
Cooking time: 25 min.

- Remove the stems and seed the **bell peppers**; thinly slice the flesh. Peel and thinly slice the **garlic** and **onions**. Cut the **chorizo** into thick rounds.
- In a pot over low heat with the **oil**, cook all the ingredients for 25 minutes, stirring occasionally, or until the vegetables are softened and the **chorizo** is browned. Add salt and pepper; serve.

SCALLOPED POTATOES WITH ANDOUILLE

Potatoes
x 2 (large)

Andouille sausages (or other similar hot link sausages)
5 ounces (150 g)

Heavy cream
Just over ¾ cup (200 mL)

**Grated cheese
(such as Gruyère)**
1¾ ounces (50 g)

 Pepper

**Preparation time: 10 min.
Cooking time: 40 min.**

- Preheat the oven to 350°F/180°C.
- Peel and thinly slice the **potatoes**. Arrange them overlapping with the **sausage** slices in a baking dish. Pour the **cream** over the top. Add the **cheese** and pepper, and bake for 40 minutes, or until browned on top.
- Serve from the baking dish.

TOMATOES STUFFED WITH SAUSAGE AND LEMONGRASS

Tomatoes
x 8

Lemongrass
4 stalks

Ground sausage
1 lb (450 g)

Nuoc-mam fish sauce
4 tbsp (60 mL)

Preparation time: 5 min.
Cooking time: 25 min.

- Preheat the oven to 400°F/210°C.
- Cut the tops off the **tomatoes** and scoop out the flesh. Finely chop the **lemongrass**. Combine the **sausage** with the **nuoc-mam** and the **lemongrass**.
- Spoon this mixture into the **tomatoes** and replace the tops. Bake for 25 minutes, or until browned and the **sausage** is cooked through; serve.

EGGPLANT PARMIGIANA

Eggplants
x 2

Tomatoes
x 4

Fresh mozzarella cheese
2 balls (8 ounces/227 g each)

**Grated cheese
(such as Gruyère)**
1¾ ounces (50 g)

👤👤👤👤

🧂 **Pepper**

🕐

**Preparation time: 5 min.
Cooking time: 40 min.**

- Preheat the oven to 400°F/210°C.
- Halve the **eggplants** lengthwise and the **tomatoes** and **mozzarella** balls crosswise; thinly slice them. Alternate them, overlapping, in a baking dish.
- Add pepper and sprinkle the **grated cheese** on top.
- Bake for 40 minutes, or until browned on top and the **cheese** is melted.

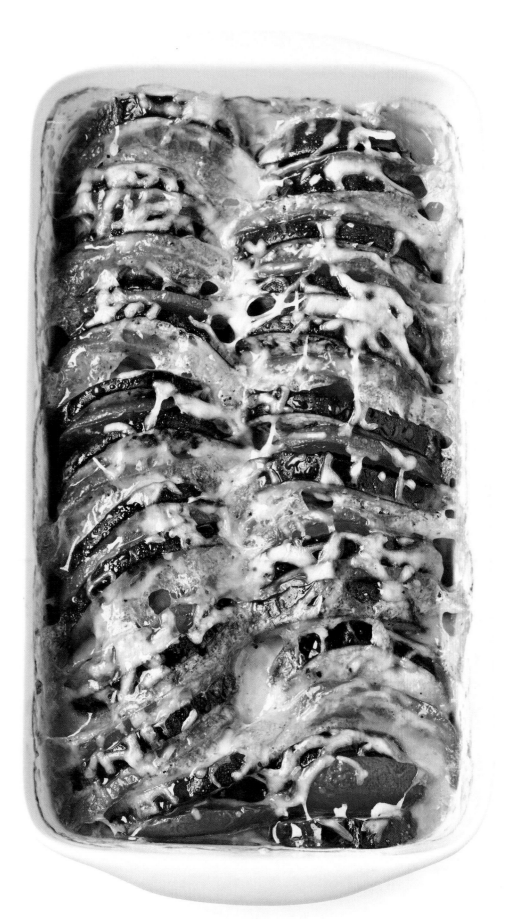

CHEESE SOUFFLÉ

Unsalted butter
4 tbsp (2⅛ ounces/60 g)

All-purpose flour
9 tbsp (2⅛ ounces/60 g)

Whole milk
1⅔ cups (400 mL)

Eggs
x 4 (separated)

**Grated cheese
(such as Gruyère)**
5¼ ounces (150 g)

**Preparation time: 15 min.
Cooking time: 35 min.**

- Preheat the oven to 350°F/180°C.
- In a saucepan, melt the **butter**, then add the **flour** and stir to thoroughly combine until smooth. Add the **milk**.
- Cook for 1 minute while stirring. Add the **egg** yolks and the **cheese**; stir to thoroughly combine. Remove from the heat.
- Using an electric mixer, beat the **egg** whites into stiff peaks. Fold them into the mixture, then pour this mixture into a large soufflé dish with high sides.
- Bake for 30 minutes, or until puffed and browned on top; serve immediately.

CHICKEN AND PEANUT DUMPLINGS

Chicken breasts
x 2

Peanut butter
2 tbsp (1¼ ounces/34 g)

Cucumber
x ¼ (about 4¼ ounces/120 g)

Spring roll wrappers
x 4 (large)

Basil
x 1 bunch

Peanuts
2 tbsp (½ oz/18 g)

👤👤👤👤

Drizzle of soy sauce

🕐

Preparation time: 15 min.
Cooking time: 5 min.

- Cube the **chicken**. In a covered microwave-safe dish, microwave the **chicken** with the **peanut butter** for 5 minutes, or until the **chicken** is cooked through; let cool.
- Dice the **cucumber**, then add it to the dish.
- Lightly moisten the **spring roll wrappers** with cold water and place them on a work surface, smooth-side down. Spoon the chicken mixture into the center of each **wrapper** and add some **basil** leaves on top; fold the **wrappers** closed.
- Chop the **peanuts**. Top the dumplings with the remaining **basil** leaves, a sprinkle of **peanuts**, and a drizzle of soy sauce.

BEEF SAUTÉED WITH LEMONGRASS

Beef tenderloin
1⅓ lb (600 g)

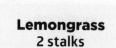

Lemongrass
2 stalks

Sweetened soy sauce
6 tbsp (90 mL)

Peanuts
2 tbsp (½ oz/18 g)

Cilantro
1 bunch

👤👤👤👤

🫗 **5 tbsp (75 mL)
flavorless cooking oil**

🕐

**Marinating: 1 hr.
Cooking time: 5 min.**

- Slice the **beef**. Finely chop the **lemongrass**. Combine the **soy sauce**, **lemongrass**, and **beef** slices with the oil. Let marinate for 1 hour.
- Just before serving, sauté the **beef** with the marinade liquid in a hot pan for 5 minutes, or until the **beef** is browned. Meanwhile, crush the **peanuts**.
- Off the heat, stir in the **cilantro** leaves and **peanuts**; serve.

THAI-STYLE BEEF TARTARE

Lemongrass
2 stalks

Thai basil
1 bunch

Soy sauce
2 tbsp (30 mL)

Sesame seeds
2 tbsp (½ oz/18 g)

Sesame oil
4 tbsp (60 mL)

Freshly ground beef
1⅓ lb (600 g)

Salt, pepper

Preparation time: 5 min.

- Finely dice the **lemongrass** and chop the **basil** (set aside a few leaves for serving).
- Thoroughly combine all the remaining ingredients with the **ground beef**; add salt and pepper.
- Divide among serving plates and serve immediately.

BEEF MEATBALLS WITH BASIL

Ground beef
1⅛ lb (500 g)

Garlic powder
1 tbsp

Sweetened soy sauce
4 tbsp (60 mL)

Basil
1 bunch

👤👤👤👤

🧂🧂 Salt, pepper

🫙 1 tbsp (15 mL)
flavorless cooking oil

⏱

Preparation time: 5 min.
Cooking time: 2 min.

• Combine the **ground beef** with the **garlic powder**. Add salt and pepper. Roll the **ground beef** into 20 meatballs and cook them over high heat in a skillet with the oil and **soy sauce** for 2 minutes, or until cooked through.
• Let cool slightly, then add **basil** leaves and stir to combine. Serve immediately.

BEEF AND COMTÉ YAKITORI

Comté cheese wedge
10½ ounces (300 g)

Beef carpaccio
14 ounces (400 g)

Sweetened soy sauce
½ cup (120 mL)

Peanuts
2 tbsp (½ oz/18 g)

Preparation time: 5 min.
Cooking time: 15 min.

- Slice the **cheese** crosswise into 8 pieces. Slice the **beef**.
- Wrap the **cheese** pieces in the **beef** slices, then skewer them. Place them in a baking dish, brush with the **soy sauce**, and bake for 15 minutes, or until the **cheese** is slightly melted and the **beef** is cooked to the desired temperature.
- Crush the **peanuts** and sprinkle them over the top; serve.

BEEF CHILI

Beef stew meat
1¾ lb (800 g)

Ground cumin
2 tbsp

Tomato purée
2 cups (500 mL)

Chile pepper purée
1 tsp

Red kidney beans
1 large can (1¾ lb/800 g), drained

👤👤👤👤

🧂🧂 **Salt, pepper**

🫙 **1 tbsp (15 mL)**
flavorless cooking oil

⏲

Preparation time: 5 min.
Cooking time: 3 hr. 30 min.

• In a large heavy pot over medium heat, brown the **beef** in the oil. Add the **cumin**, **tomato** and **chile pepper purées**, and 3⅓ cups (800 mL) of water. Cook for 3 hours over very low heat, covered, stirring occasionally.

• After the cooking time, add the **beans**, stir to combine, and cook for 30 more minutes, uncovered, or until the **beef** is cooked through and the **beans** are tender; serve.

CHILI RAPIDO

Red kidney beans
1 large can (1¾ lb/800 g), drained

Ground beef
9 ounces (250 g)

Tomato purée
1 cup (250 mL)

Ground cumin
1 tbsp

Grated Cheddar cheese
3½ ounces (100 g)

 Salt, pepper

Preparation time: 5 min.
Cooking time: 12 min.

• In a microwave-safe dish, combine the **beans** with the **ground beef**, a dash of salt and pepper, **tomato purée**, **cumin**, half the **Cheddar**, and just over ¾ cup (200 mL) of water.

• Top with the remaining **Cheddar** and microwave uncovered for 12 minutes (at 800 watts), or just until the **cheese** is melted and the **beef** is cooked through; serve.

BEEF CHEEKS WITH LEMONGRASS

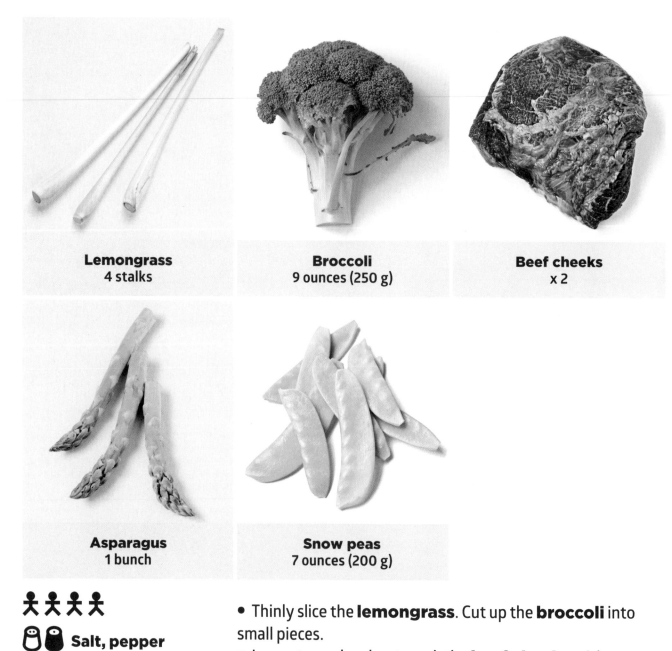

Lemongrass
4 stalks

Broccoli
9 ounces (250 g)

Beef cheeks
x 2

Asparagus
1 bunch

Snow peas
7 ounces (200 g)

Salt, pepper

Preparation time: 5 min.
Cooking time: 2 hr.

- Thinly slice the **lemongrass**. Cut up the **broccoli** into small pieces.
- In a pot over low heat, cook the **beef cheeks** with the **lemongrass** and 2 quarts (2 L) of water for 1 hour 45 minutes.
- Add the **broccoli**, **asparagus** (tough stem ends removed), and the **snow peas**. Add salt and pepper and cook for 10 to 15 minutes, or until the **beef** and vegetables are cooked through.

RIB EYE STEAK IN RED WINE AND SHALLOT SAUCE

Shallots
x 10

Red wine
½ bottle (375 mL)

**Bouquets garnis
(bay leaf, thyme)**
x 2

Chicken broth
Just over ¾ cup (200 mL)

Boneless rib eye steaks
x 4 (6⅔ ounces/190 g each)

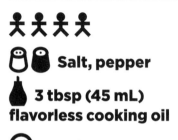

Salt, pepper

**3 tbsp (45 mL)
flavorless cooking oil**

**Preparation time: 10 min.
Cooking time: 45 min.**

• Peel and thinly slice the **shallots**. In a skillet with 2 tbsp (30 mL) of the **oil**, cook the shallots for 5 minutes, or until lightly browned. Add the **wine**, **bouquets garnis**, and **broth**. Let cook for about 40 minutes over low heat until slightly reduced.

• Sear the **steaks** in the remaining oil in a separate skillet over high heat for 2 minutes on each side, or until cooked to the desired doneness. Remove from the heat, brush with the sauce, and add salt and pepper. Serve immediately.

HERBED BONE-IN RIB EYE

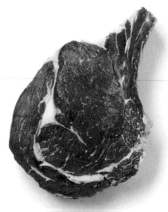

Bone-in rib eye steak
x 1 (about 3 lb/1.3 kg)

Rosemary
4 sprigs

Thyme
4 sprigs

🧍🧍🧍🧍

🧂 **Salt, pepper**

🫗 **2 tbsp (30 mL) extra-virgin olive oil**

🕐

Preparation time: 5 min.
Cooking time: 24 min.
Resting time: 5 min.

- Preheat the oven to 400°F/210°C.
- In a skillet over high heat with the oil, sear the **steak** for 2 minutes on each side.
- Transfer the **steak** to a baking dish and add the herbs. Add salt and pepper and bake for 20 minutes, or until cooked to the desired doneness, basting occasionally with the cooking juices.
- Let rest for 5 minutes, turning once, then serve immediately.

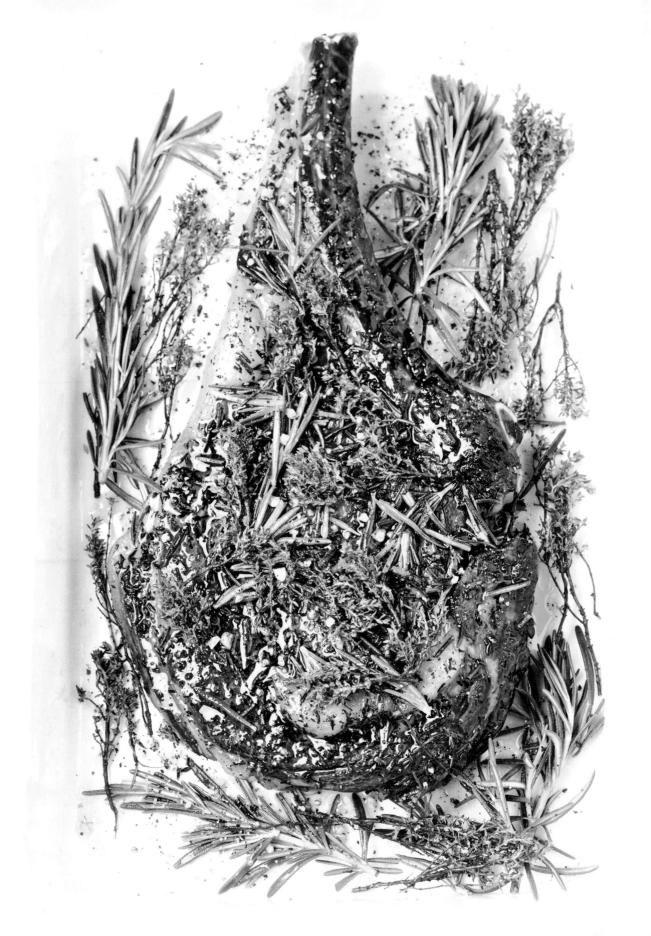

VENISON AND CHANTERELLES

Venison tournedos
x 4

Trumpet chanterelle mushrooms
9 ounces (250 g)

Soy sauce
2 tbsp (30 mL)

Heavy cream
Just over ¾ cup (200 mL)

Fresh raspberries
9 ounces (250 g)

👫👫

🧂🧂 **Salt, pepper**

🫗 **1 tbsp (15 mL) flavorless cooking oil**

🕐

Preparation time: 5 min.
Cooking time: 5 min.

- Remove any fat from around the **venison**, then cube the meat.
- Sear the **meat** on both sides in a skillet over high heat with the oil; let cook for 1 minute. Add the **mushrooms**, **soy sauce**, **cream**, and **raspberries**. Cook for 1 more minute, or until the meat is cooked to the desired doneness. Add salt and pepper; serve.

LEG OF VENISON IN WINE SAUCE

Leg of venison
x 1 (3⅓ lb/1.5 kg)

Red wine
2 cups (500 mL)

Rosemary
2 sprigs

**Bouquets garnis
(bay leaf, thyme)**
x 3

Unsweetened cocoa powder
2 tbsp (⅓ oz/10 g)

Coarse-ground peppercorns
1 tbsp (⅓ oz/10 g)

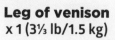

Salt

Preparation time: 15 min.
Marinating: 1 hr.
Cooking time: 50 min.

- Preheat the oven to 350°F/180°C.
- Marinate the **venison** for 1 hour in the **wine**, **rosemary**, and **bouquets garnis**.
- Transfer the **venison** to a large baking dish and sprinkle it with the **cocoa powder** and **peppercorns**. Add salt.
- Heat the marinade liquid in a saucepan for 5 minutes. Pour the liquid over the **venison** and bake for 45 minutes, or until the meat is cooked to the desired doneness, basting frequently with the cooking juices; serve.

QUAIL BOURGUIGNON

Quail
x 4

Red onion
x 1

Red wine
4¼ cups (1 L)

Ruby port
2 cups (500 mL)

**Bouquets garnis
(bay leaf, thyme)**
x 4

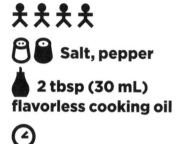

Salt, pepper

**2 tbsp (30 mL)
flavorless cooking oil**

②

**Preparation time: 5 min.
Cooking time: 1 hr. 2 min.**

- In a large heavy pot over high heat with the oil, cook the **quail** for 2 minutes, or until lightly browned on all sides.
- Peel and chop the **onion**. Add the **wine**, **port**, **onion**, and **bouquets garnis** to the pot. Add salt and pepper. Cook for 1 hour over low heat, uncovered, stirring occasionally, or until the **quail** are cooked through; serve.

COOKED RABBIT TERRINE

Rabbit
x 1 (cut up)

White wine
1⅔ cups (400 mL)

Sun-dried tomatoes
x 10

Tarragon
1 bunch

Rustic bread
8 slices

👤👤👤👤

🧂🧂 **Salt, pepper**

🕐

Preparation time: 5 min.
Cooking time: 1 hr.
Refrigeration: Overnight

• The night before, in a large heavy pot over low heat, cook the **rabbit**, **wine**, **tomatoes**, and 1⅔ cups (400 mL) of water for 1 hour, or until the **rabbit** is cooked through. Shred the meat and strain and reserve the cooking liquid. Combine the **tomatoes**, meat, and cooking liquid, then transfer this mixture to a terrine. Refrigerate overnight, to thicken.
• The next day, chop the **tarragon** and add it to the terrine. Add salt and pepper to taste. Grill the **bread** slices and serve.

PHEASANT STEW

Shallots
x 2

White button mushrooms
9 ounces (250 g)

Pheasant
x 1 (cleaned and cut up)

Bacon lardons
7 ounces (200 g)

Chicken broth
2 cups (500 mL)

👤👤👤👤

🧂🧂 **Salt, pepper**

🫗 **2 tbsp (30 mL) flavorless cooking oil**

🕐

Preparation time: 10 min.
Cooking time: 1 hr. 5 min.

• Chop the **shallots** and the **mushrooms**.
• In a large heavy pot with the **oil**, brown the **pheasant** pieces. Add the **shallots**, **mushrooms**, **lardons**, and **broth**. Add salt and pepper and let simmer for 1 hour over very low heat, covered, or until the **pheasant** is cooked through and the vegetables are tender; serve.

BAKED RABBIT WITH ROSEMARY AND TOMATOES

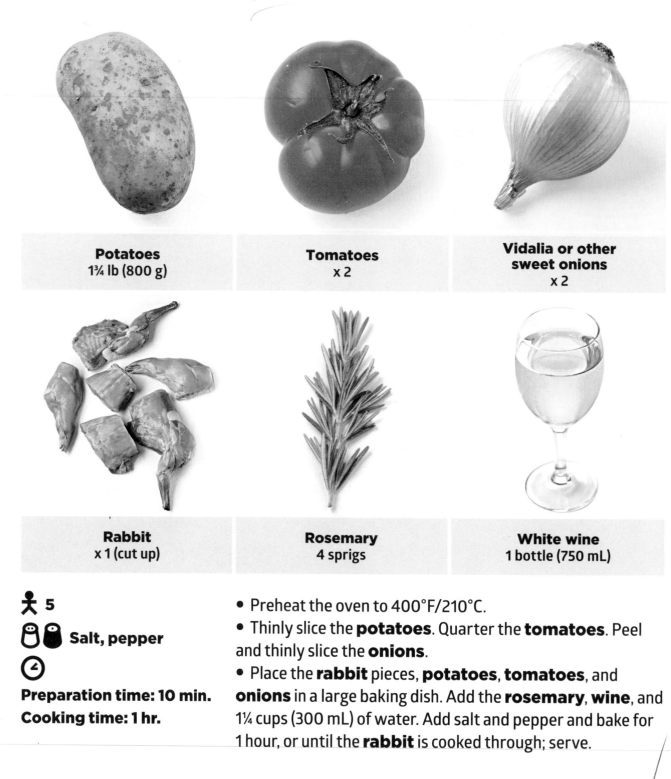

Potatoes
1¾ lb (800 g)

Tomatoes
x 2

Vidalia or other sweet onions
x 2

Rabbit
x 1 (cut up)

Rosemary
4 sprigs

White wine
1 bottle (750 mL)

👤 5

🧂🧂 Salt, pepper

🕐

Preparation time: 10 min.
Cooking time: 1 hr.

- Preheat the oven to 400°F/210°C.
- Thinly slice the **potatoes**. Quarter the **tomatoes**. Peel and thinly slice the **onions**.
- Place the **rabbit** pieces, **potatoes**, **tomatoes**, and **onions** in a large baking dish. Add the **rosemary**, **wine**, and 1¼ cups (300 mL) of water. Add salt and pepper and bake for 1 hour, or until the **rabbit** is cooked through; serve.

COCONUT, SAFFRON, AND BASIL CHICKEN

Coconut milk
2 cups (500 mL)

Saffron threads
3 small pinches

Basil
1 bunch

Chicken legs
x 4

👤👤👤👤

🧂🧂 **Salt, pepper**

🕐

Preparation time: 5 min.
Cooking time: 45 min.

• Preheat the oven to 400°F/210°C.
• Whisk together the **coconut milk** and **saffron**. Add the **basil** leaves.
• Place the **chicken legs** in a baking dish and pour the coconut milk–saffron mixture on top. Add salt and pepper and bake for 45 minutes, or until the **chicken** is cooked through; serve.

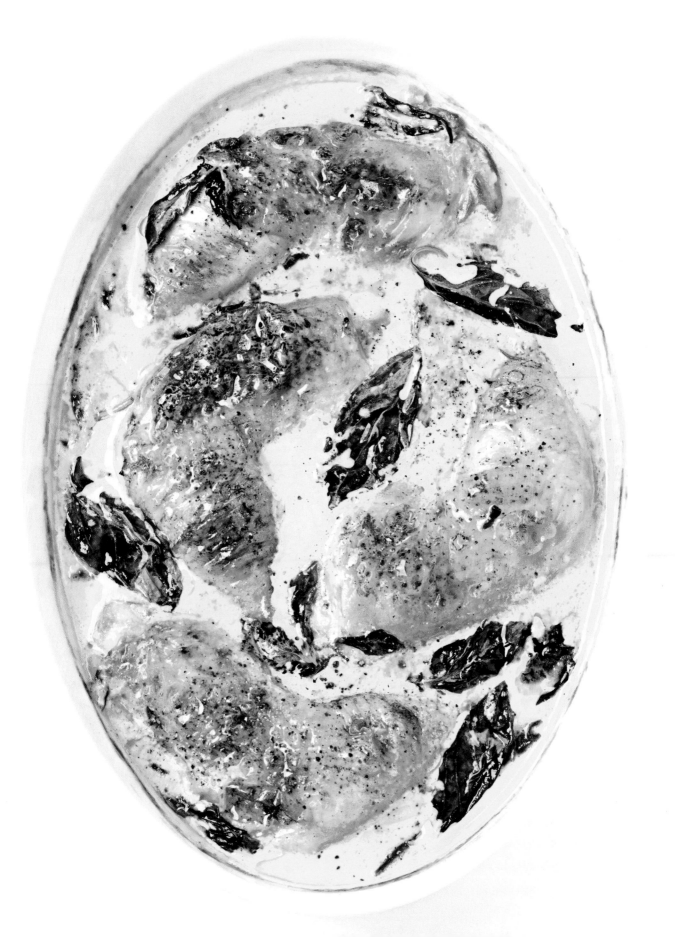

TURKEY SATAY

Turkey cutlets
x 4

Peanut butter
4 tbsp (2½ ounces/68 g)

Honey
2 tbsp (30 mL)

Soy sauce
4 tbsp (60 mL)

Preparation time: 5 min.
Cooking time: 20 min.

- Preheat the oven to 400°F/210°C.
- Cut the **turkey** cutlets into bite-size pieces. Combine the **peanut butter** and **honey**, then coat the **turkey** pieces in this mixture and skewer them.
- Place the skewers in a baking dish and add the **soy sauce** and just over ¾ cup (200 mL) of water. Bake for 20 minutes, or until the **turkey** is cooked through; serve.

TURKEY LEGS WITH BELL PEPPERS

Rosemary
4 sprigs

Turkey legs
x 4

Assorted bell peppers
x 6

Garlic
12 cloves (unpeeled)

Extra-virgin olive oil
4 tbsp (60 mL)

Salt, pepper

Preparation time: 10 min.
Cooking time: 1 hr.

• Preheat the oven to 400°F/210°C.
• Tuck half the **rosemary** under the skin of the **turkey** legs, then place the leg in a large baking dish.
• Remove the stems and seed the **bell peppers**; chop the flesh. Add the **bell peppers**, **garlic**, remaining **rosemary**, **oil**, and just over ¾ cup (200 mL) of water to the dish. Add salt and pepper and bake for 1 hour, or until the **turkey** is cooked through, basting occasionally with the cooking juices; serve.

BAKED CRISPY CHICKEN DRUMSTICKS

Chicken drumsticks
x 8

Barbecue sauce
6 tbsp (90 mL)

Eggs
x 3

All-purpose flour
1 cup (3½ ounces/100 g)

Cornflakes
x 10 handfuls (4¼ ounces/120 g)

🧍🧍🧍🧍

🧂🧂 **Salt, pepper**

🕐

Preparation time: 15 min.
Marinating: 10 min.
Cooking time: 45 min.

- Preheat the oven to 350°F/180°C.
- Salt and pepper the **drumsticks**, then coat them in 2 tbsp (30 mL) of the **barbecue sauce**; let marinate for 10 minutes.
- In a bowl, lightly beat the **eggs** with a fork. Dredge the **drumsticks** in the **flour**, then in the **eggs**. Lightly crush the **cornflakes**. Coat the **drumsticks** in the **cornflakes** and place them in a baking dish. Bake for 45 minutes, or until cooked through. Serve with the remaining **barbecue sauce**.

ITALIAN-STYLE TURKEY CUTLETS

Tomato
x 1

Fresh mozzarella cheese
2 balls (8 ounces/227 g each)

Basil
8 leaves

Turkey cutlets
x 4

Grated Parmesan cheese
4 tbsp (½ oz/12 g)

 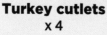 

👥👥👥👥

🧂 **Salt, pepper**

🫗 **Drizzle of extra-virgin olive oil**

🕐

Preparation time: 5 min.
Cooking time: 20 min.

- Preheat the oven to 400°F/210°C.
- Cut the **tomato** into 4 wedges. Halve the **mozzarella** balls.
- Place a half of a **mozzarella** ball, 2 **basil** leaves, and 1 wedge of **tomato** on top of each **turkey** cutlet. Add salt and pepper, then roll up the cutlets, securing them with toothpicks. Sprinkle with the **Parmesan** and bake for 20 minutes, or until the **cheese** is melted and golden and the **turkey** is cooked through. Serve, drizzled with oil.

COCONUT AND PESTO CHICKEN

Chicken legs
x 4 (halved at the joint)

Coconut milk
1 cup (250 mL)

Pesto
2 tbsp (30 mL)

👤👤👤👤

🧂🧂 **Salt, pepper**

⏱

Preparation time: 5 min.
Cooking time: 45 min.

- Preheat the oven to 350°F/180°C.
- Place the **chicken** pieces in a baking dish and add the **coconut milk**. Spread the **pesto** on top of the **chicken**. Bake for 45 minutes, or until the **chicken** is cooked through. Add salt and pepper; serve.

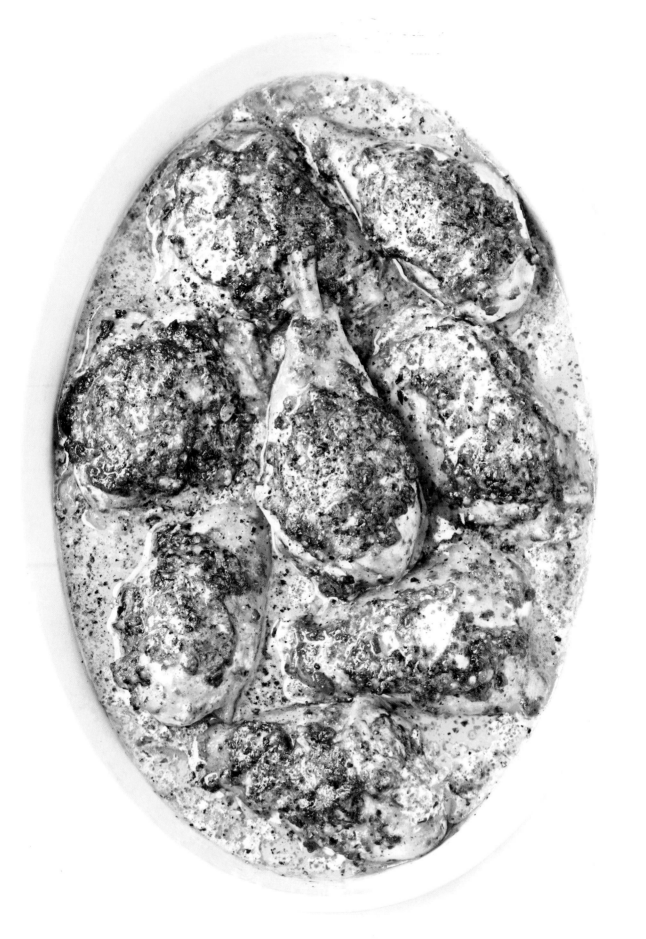

SWEET AND SOUR CHICKEN WINGS

Chicken wings
x 16

Ketchup
4 tbsp (60 mL)

Soy sauce
6 tbsp (90 mL)

Honey
4 tbsp (60 mL)

Preparation time: 5 min.
Cooking time: 45 min.

- Preheat the oven to 400°F/210°C.
- Place the **chicken wings** in a baking dish and brush them with a mixture of 2 tbsp (30 mL) of the **ketchup**, 4 tbsp (60 mL) of the **soy sauce**, and 2 tbsp (30 mL) of the **honey**. Bake for 45 minutes, or until the **wings** are cooked through.
- Combine the remaining **ketchup**, **soy sauce**, and **honey** and serve this as a sauce on the side.

GINGER CHICKEN

Chicken breasts
x 4

Fresh ginger
1¾ ounces (50 g)

Yellow curry powder
1 tbsp

Sweetened soy sauce
4 tbsp (60 mL) + more for serving

Cilantro
1 bunch

👤👤👤👤

🫗 **1 tbsp (15 mL) flavorless cooking oil**

🕐

Preparation time: 5 min.
Marinating: 1 hr.
Cooking time: 5 min.

• Chop the **chicken breasts**. Peel and grate the **ginger**. Combine the **chicken** with the **ginger**, **curry powder**, **soy sauce**, and **oil** and let marinate for 1 hour.

• In a skillet over high heat, sauté the **chicken** in the marinade liquid for 5 minutes, or until the **chicken** is cooked through.

• Off the heat, stir in the **cilantro** leaves; serve, with **soy sauce** on the side.

CHICKEN ROULADES À L'ORANGE

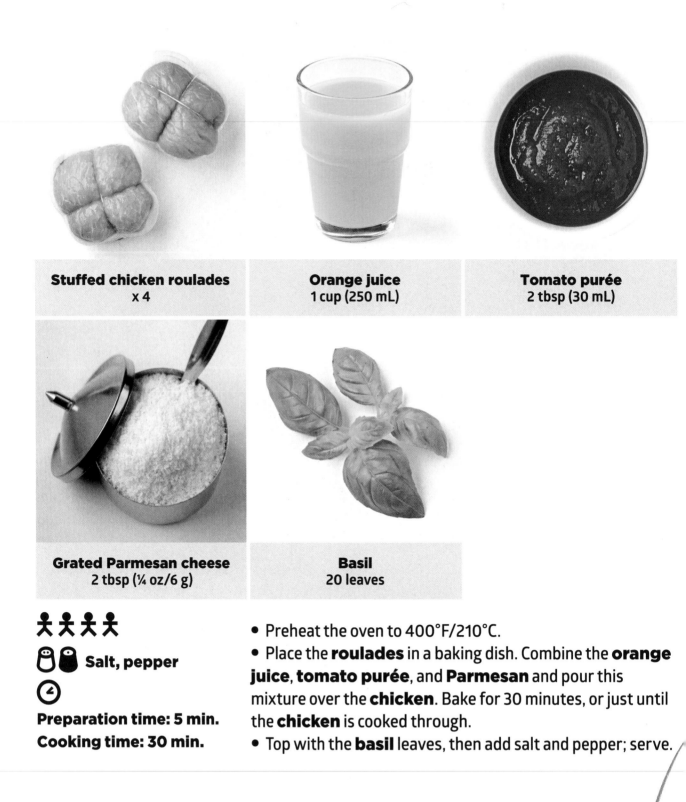

Stuffed chicken roulades
x 4

Orange juice
1 cup (250 mL)

Tomato purée
2 tbsp (30 mL)

Grated Parmesan cheese
2 tbsp (¼ oz/6 g)

Basil
20 leaves

Salt, pepper

Preparation time: 5 min.
Cooking time: 30 min.

- Preheat the oven to 400°F/210°C.
- Place the **roulades** in a baking dish. Combine the **orange juice**, **tomato purée**, and **Parmesan** and pour this mixture over the **chicken**. Bake for 30 minutes, or just until the **chicken** is cooked through.
- Top with the **basil** leaves, then add salt and pepper; serve.

PROSCIUTTO-WRAPPED GUINEA HEN WITH POTATOES

Potatoes
1¾ lb (800 g)

Vidalia or other sweet onions
x 2

Guinea hen legs
x 4

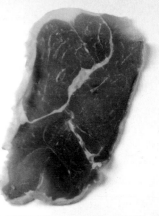

Prosciutto
4 slices

Chicken broth
4¼ cups (1 L)

**Bouquets garnis
(bay leaf, thyme)**
x 3

👤👤👤👤

🧂🧂 Salt, pepper

🫒 Drizzle of extra-virgin olive oil

②

**Preparation time: 10 min.
Cooking time: 1 hr.**

- Preheat the oven to 350°F/180°C.
- Peel and thinly slice the **potatoes** and **onions** and place them in a baking dish.
- Wrap each **guinea hen leg** in 1 slice of **prosciutto**, then add them to the dish with the **broth** and **bouquets garnis**. Add salt and pepper, drizzle with oil, and bake for 1 hour, or until the legs are cooked through and the **potatoes** are tender; serve.

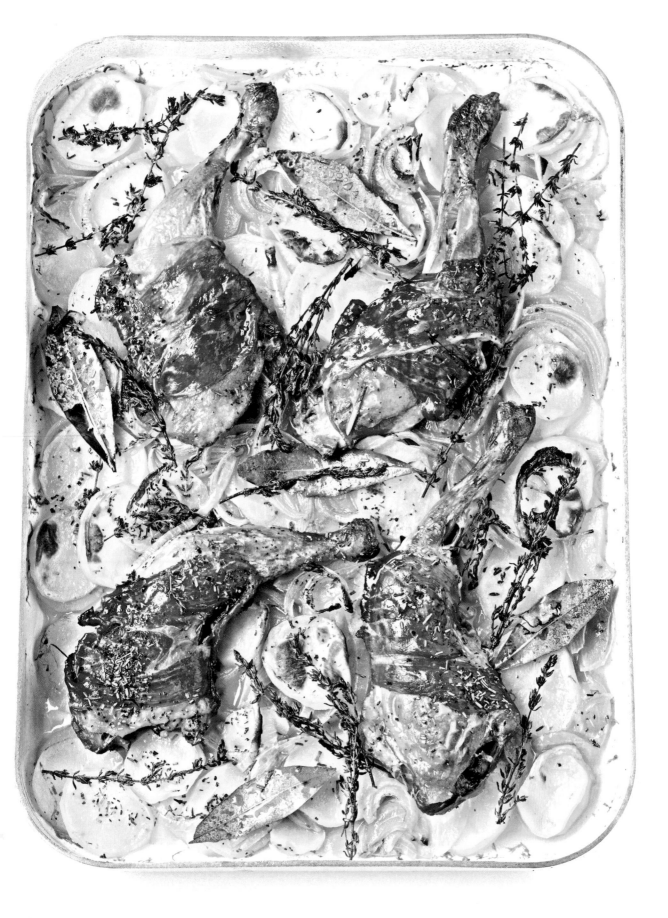

MANGO-CURRY CHICKEN

Coconut milk
1⅔ cups (400 mL)

Yellow curry powder
1 tbsp

Chicken breasts
x 4

Mango
x 1

Cilantro
1 bunch

Frozen peas
5¼ ounces (150 g), thawed

Preparation time: 5 min.
Cooking time: 25 min.

- Preheat the oven to 350°F/180°C.
- In a saucepan, whisk together the **coconut milk** and **curry powder** and bring to a boil.
- Chop the **chicken**. Place the **chicken** pieces in a baking dish and pour the hot coconut milk–curry mixture over the top. Bake for 20 minutes, or until the **chicken** is cooked through.
- Peel and dice the **mango**. Chop the **cilantro**. Combine the **mango**, **cilantro**, and **peas**, then stir this mixture into the hot dish; serve.

CHICKEN WITH OLIVES

Olive tapenade
2 tbsp (30 mL)

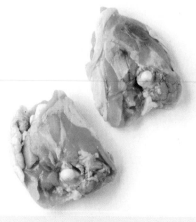

Chicken thighs
x 4

Tomatoes
x 2

Preparation time: 5 min.
Cooking time: 40 min.

- Preheat the oven to 400°F/210°C.
- Combine the **tapenade** with just over ¾ cup (200 mL) of water. Place the **thighs** in a baking dish. Pour the tapenade mixture over the top.
- Cut the **tomato** into wedges and add them to the dish. Bake for 40 minutes, or until the **chicken** is cooked through; serve.

244

LIME AND ROSEMARY CHICKEN

Organic limes
x 2

Fresh mozzarella cheese
1 ball (8 ounces/227 g)

Chicken breasts
x 4

Rosemary
2 sprigs

Extra-virgin olive oil
2 tbsp (30 mL)

👤👤👤👤

🧂 **Salt, pepper**

🕐

Preparation time: 5 min.
Cooking time: 30 min.

- Preheat the oven to 350°F/180°C.
- Zest and juice 1 of the **limes**, then slice the remaining **lime**. Slice the **mozzarella**.
- Place the **chicken breasts** in a baking dish. Add the **mozzarella** and **lime** slices, **rosemary**, and the **lime** zest and juice. Add salt and pepper, drizzle with the **oil**, and bake for 30 minutes, or until the **chicken** is cooked through; serve immediately.

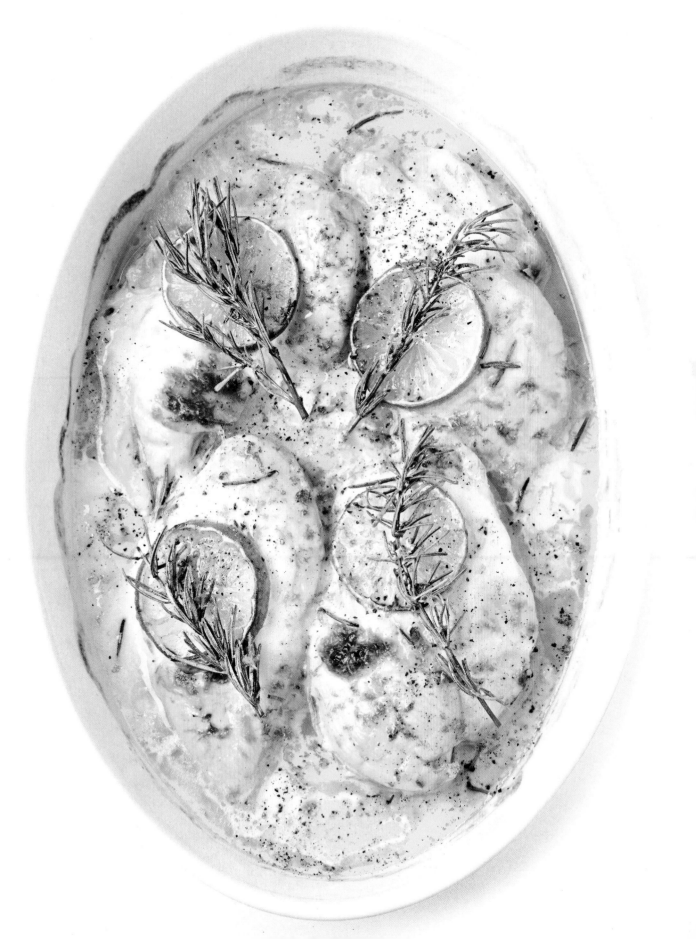

WHOLE ROAST CHICKEN ON BREAD

Rustic bread
4 thick slices

Whole chicken
x 1 (trussed)

Garlic
8 cloves (unpeeled)

Shallots
x 4 (unpeeled)

**Bouquets garnis
(bay leaf, thyme)**
x 3

 Salt, pepper

Drizzle of extra-virgin olive oil

Preparation time: 5 min.
Cooking time: 1 hr.

- Preheat the oven to 325°F/170°C.
- Cover the bottom of a baking dish with the **bread** slices and place the **chicken** on top, breast-side up. Add the **garlic**, **shallots**, and the **bouquets garnis**. Add a drizzle of oil, sprinkle with salt and pepper, and bake for 1 hour, or until the **chicken** is cooked through.
- Serve the **chicken** with the moist **bread** slices.

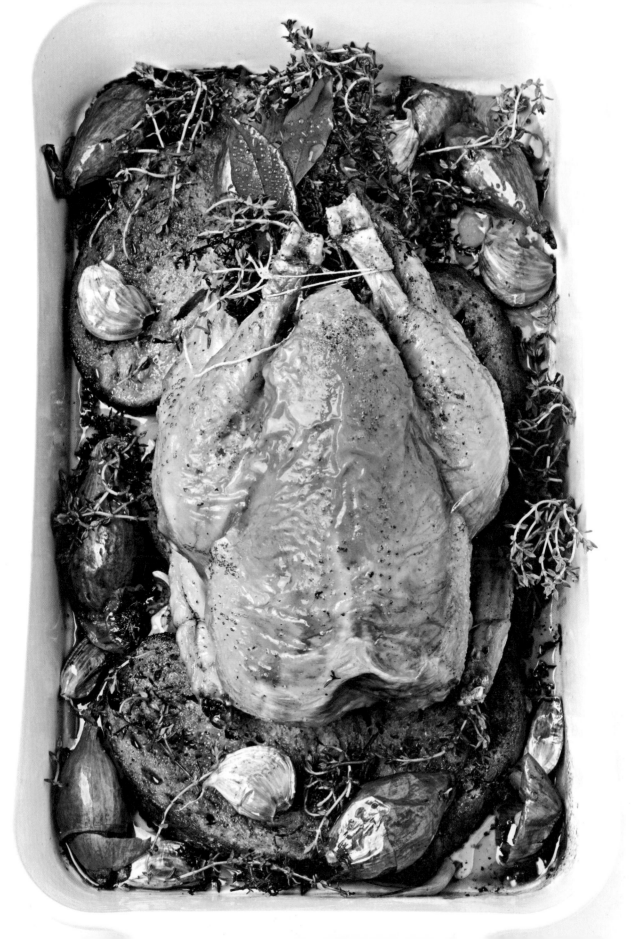

DUCK BREASTS WITH BASIL AND GINGER

Fresh ginger
2⅛ ounces (60 g)

Duck breasts
x 2 (1⅛ lb/500 g total)

Soy sauce
6 tbsp (90 mL)

Thai basil
1 bunch

👤👤👤👤

🧂 Pepper

🕐

Preparation time: 5 min.
Cooking time: 7 min.

• Peel and grate the **ginger**. Cut up the **duck breasts**, keeping any pieces of fat attached, and brown the pieces in a dry skillet with the **ginger** for 2 minutes. Add the **soy sauce** and cook for 5 minutes, or until the **duck** reaches the desired doneness.

• Remove from the heat. Add the **basil** leaves and pepper, stir to combine, and serve immediately.

DUCK CONFIT PROVENÇAL

Tomatoes
x 4

**Bouquets garnis
(bay leaf, thyme)**
x 2

**Black olives
(Greek marinated)**
x 20

Duck-legs confit
x 4

**Preparation time: 5 min.
Cooking time: 45 min.**

- Preheat the oven to 325°F/170°C.
- Dice the **tomatoes** and place them in a baking dish with the **bouquets garnis** and **olives**. Place the **duck legs** in the dish and bake for 45 minutes, or until the **duck** skin is browned and the meat is cooked to the desired doneness. Serve very hot.

DUCK LEGS WITH TURNIPS AND OLIVES

Golden ball turnips
x 8

Duck legs
x 4

Olive tapenade
2 tbsp (30 mL)

👤👤👤👤

🧂🧂 **Salt, pepper**

🕐

Preparation time: 10 min.
Cooking time: 2 hr.

• Peel and chop the **turnips**. Place the **duck legs** and **turnips** in a pot with 4¼ cups (1 L) of water and cook for 2 hours over low heat, covered, or until the **duck** reaches the desired doneness.

• Add the **tapenade**, sprinkle with salt and pepper, and stir to combine. Transfer to a serving dish and serve immediately.

DUCK BREASTS À L'ORANGE

Organic oranges
x 5

Honey
4 tbsp (60 mL)

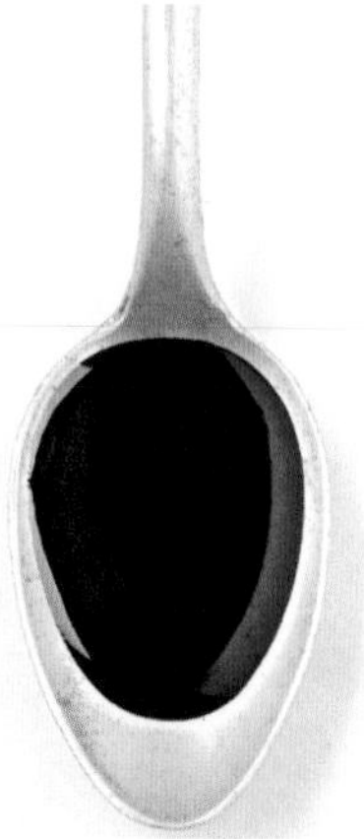

Balsamic vinegar
5 tbsp (75 mL)

Duck breasts
x 2 (1⅛ lb/500 g total)

Preparation time: 5 min.
Cooking time: 16 min.
Resting time: 5 min.

- Juice 4 of the **oranges**. Slice the remaining **orange**. In a saucepan, bring the **orange** juice and slices, **honey**, and **vinegar** to a boil. Cook for 10 minutes over low heat.
- In a dry skillet over high heat, sear the **duck breasts** skin-side down until browned. Turn and cook for 3 more minutes, or just until they reach the desired doneness. Remove from the heat and let rest for 5 minutes.
- Transfer the **duck** to a serving dish with the orange sauce and the slices of cooked **orange**; serve.

ASIAN-STYLE VEAL ROULADES

Stuffed veal roulades
x 5

Fresh ginger
1¾ ounces (50 g)

Lemongrass
3 stalks

Sweetened soy sauce
½ cup (120 mL)

Cilantro
1 bunch

👥 5

🧂 Pepper

🕐
Preparation time: 5 min.
Cooking time: 50 min.

- Preheat the oven to 400°F/210°C.
- Place the **veal roulades** in a baking dish.
- Peel and grate the **ginger**. Finely chop the **lemongrass**. In a saucepan, bring the **soy sauce**, **ginger**, and **lemongrass** to a boil with ⅓ cup (100 mL) of water. Pour the hot mixture over the **veal**. Add pepper and bake for 45 minutes, or until the **veal** is cooked through.
- Place **cilantro** leaves on top and serve.

SEARED VEAL CHOP IN TARRAGON CREAM

Veal chop
x 1 (thick cut, about 2 lb/900 g)

Tarragon
2 bunches

Heavy cream
1⅓ cups (330 mL)

Baby spinach
1¾ ounces (50 g)

Salt, pepper

1 tbsp (15 mL)
flavorless cooking oil

Preparation time: 5 min.
Cooking time: 25 min.

- In a heavy pot, sear the **veal chop** in the oil until browned on one side. Turn, then add salt and pepper. Cook for 12 minutes over low heat.
- Chop the **tarragon**, then add it to the pot with the **cream** and **spinach**. Cook for 3 more minutes, or until the **veal** is cooked through, basting with the cooking juices. Transfer to a serving dish and serve.

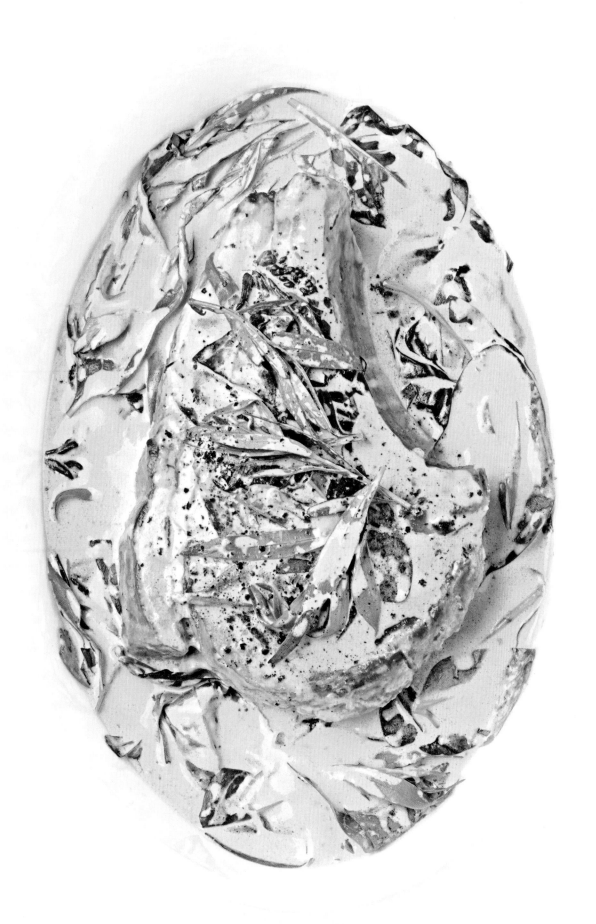

VEAL BREAST IN HONEY AND LIME

Veal breast x 4 (cut into ribs)	**Honey** 4 tbsp (60 mL)	**Soy sauce** ½ cup (120 mL)

Organic limes
x 3

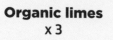

Pepper

Preparation time: 5 min.
Cooking time: 45 min.

- Preheat the oven to 400°F/210°C.
- Place the **veal breast** ribs in a large baking dish. Brush them with the **honey** and **soy sauce**.
- Zest and juice 2 of the **limes** and add this to the dish. Slice the remaining **lime** and place the slices on top of the ribs. Add pepper. Bake for 45 minutes, or until the **veal** is cooked through, basting occasionally with the cooking juices.
- Serve very hot.

VEAL CUTLETS WITH HAM AND SAGE

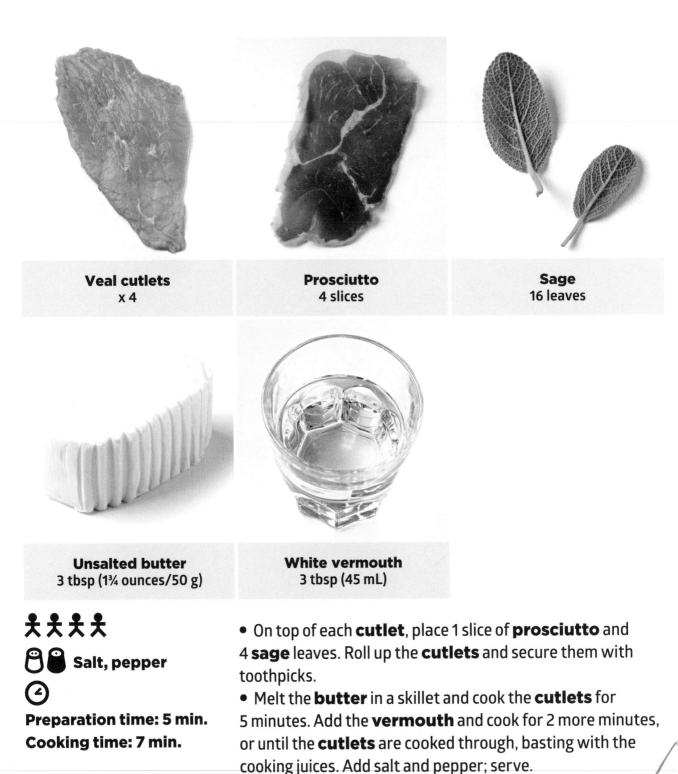

Veal cutlets
x 4

Prosciutto
4 slices

Sage
16 leaves

Unsalted butter
3 tbsp (1¾ ounces/50 g)

White vermouth
3 tbsp (45 mL)

Salt, pepper

Preparation time: 5 min.
Cooking time: 7 min.

• On top of each **cutlet**, place 1 slice of **prosciutto** and 4 **sage** leaves. Roll up the **cutlets** and secure them with toothpicks.
• Melt the **butter** in a skillet and cook the **cutlets** for 5 minutes. Add the **vermouth** and cook for 2 more minutes, or until the **cutlets** are cooked through, basting with the cooking juices. Add salt and pepper; serve.

SAUTÉED VEAL CUTLETS WITH PEANUTS

Veal cutlets
x 4

Honey
4 tbsp (60 mL)

Soy sauce
1 cup (250 mL)

Peanuts
½ cup (2½ ounces/72 g)

👤👤👤👤

🍶 **2 tbsp (30 mL)
flavorless cooking oil**

🕐

**Preparation time: 2 min.
Cooking time: 5 min.**

• Slice the **cutlets**. Warm the oil in a skillet and cook the **veal** pieces for 2 minutes, or just until browned on both sides.

• Add the **honey**, **soy sauce**, and **peanuts**. Cook for 3 more minutes, stirring, or until the **veal** is cooked through; serve.

FOUR-HOUR LEG OF LAMB

Leg of lamb
x 1 (trimmed)

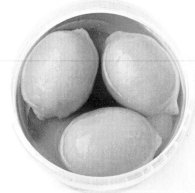

Preserved lemons
x 4

Green pitted olives
x 1 small jar (10½ ounces/300 g)

Chicken broth
4¼ cups (1 L)

Cumin seeds
1 tbsp

Honey
6 tbsp (90 mL)

👤 6

🕐
**Preparation time: 5 min.
Cooking time: 4 hr.**

- Preheat the oven to 325°F/170°C.
- Place the **lamb** in an oven-safe casserole dish. Quarter the **lemons**. Add the **lemons**, **olives**, **broth**, and **cumin seeds** to the dish. Cover and bake for 4 hours, or until the **lamb** is cooked to the desired doneness.
- Bring the **honey** to a boil in a saucepan. Out of the oven, brush the **lamb** with the warm **honey**. Serve immediately.

CURRIED LAMB CHOPS

Yellow curry powder
2 tbsp

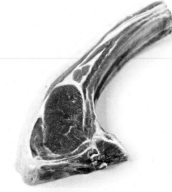

Lamb rib chops
x 8

Zucchinis
x 4 (medium)

Tomatoes
x 2

Mint
4 sprigs

👤👤👤👤

🧂🧂 Salt, pepper

🫗 6 tbsp (90 mL)
flavorless cooking oil

🕐

Preparation time: 10 min.
Marinating: 30 min.
Cooking time: 25 min.

- Combine the **curry powder** and oil. Let the **lamp chops** marinate for 30 minutes in this mixture.
- Preheat the oven to 400°F/210°C.
- Thinly slice the **zucchinis**. Slice the **tomatoes**. Place the **zucchini**, **tomatoes**, **lamb chops**, and **marinade** liquid in a baking dish. Add salt and pepper and bake for 25 minutes, or until the **lamb chops** are cooked to the desired doneness.
- Add **mint** leaves and serve.

LAMB SHANKS WITH CITRUS

Organic oranges
x 2

Organic pink grapefruit
x 1

Lamb shanks (knuckle end)
x 4

**Sauternes
(sweet white wine)**
1 bottle (750 mL)

**Bouquets garnis
(bay leaf, thyme)**
x 3

Salt, pepper

Preparation time: 5 min.
Cooking time: 4 hr.

• Preheat the oven to 350°F/180°C.
• Zest and juice the **oranges** and **grapefruit**. Place the **lamb** in an oven-safe casserole dish. Add the **wine**, **bouquets garnis**, and all the zest and juice. Bake for 4 hours, covered, or until the **lamb** is cooked to the desired doneness.
• Add salt and pepper; serve from the casserole dish.

COLOMBO SPICE LAMB

Colombo spice (or mild curry)
2 tbsp

Lamb stew meat
2¼ lb (1 kg)

Potatoes
1½ lb/700 g

👤👤👤👤

🧂🧂 **Salt, pepper**

🕐

Preparation time: 15 min.
Cooking time: 1 hr.

- Preheat the oven to 350°F/180°C.
- Combine the **spice** with 2 cups (500 mL) of water and brush the mixture over the **lamb** to coat it. Add salt and pepper.
- Peel and thinly slice the **potatoes**. Place half the **potato** slices in the bottom of a baking dish. Add the **lamb** on top with the remaining spice mixture liquid. Arrange the remaining **potatoes** around the edge of the dish. Bake for 1 hour, or until the **lamb** is cooked to the desired doneness and the **potatoes** are tender; serve immediately.

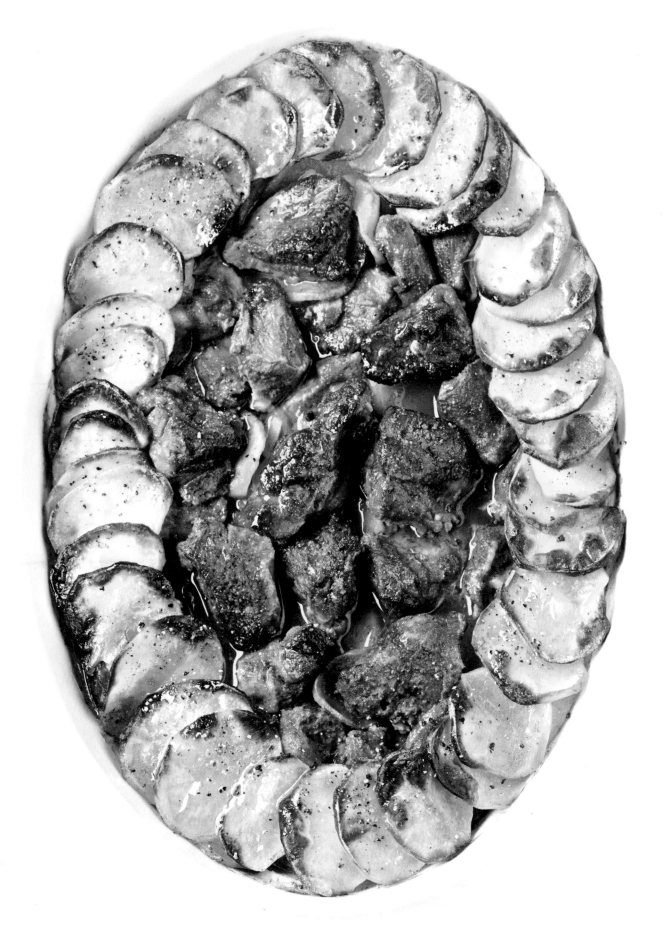

LAMB SHANKS IN HONEY

Lamb shanks (knuckle end)
x 4

Soy sauce
½ cup (120 mL)

Dried apricots
x 10

Honey
6 tbsp (90 mL)

Thyme
x 4 sprigs

👤👤👤👤

🧂🧂 **Salt, pepper**

🕐

Preparation time: 5 min.
Cooking time: 1 hr. 20 min.

• Place all the ingredients in a heavy pot with 2 cups (500 mL) of water. Bring to a boil, then lower the heat. Cook for 1 hour 15 minutes over low heat, covered, or until the **lamb** is cooked to the desired doneness, basting occasionally with the cooking juices.

• Add salt and pepper. Serve with a side of puréed potatoes, if desired.

STEWED LEG OF LAMB WITH SAFFRON

Carrots
x 4

Turnips
x 4

Leg of lamb
x 1 (boned)

**Bouquets garnis
(bay leaf, thyme)**
x 2

Saffron
15 threads (or 2 small pinches)

Coarse gray salt
1 tbsp

🧍 **4 to 5**

🧂 **Pepper**

🕐

**Preparation time: 5 min.
Cooking time: 2 hr. 30 min.**

- Peel the **carrots**. Peel and chop the **turnips**.
- Cut the **lamb** leg into 6 pieces and place them in a large heavy pot with the **carrots**, **turnips**, **bouquets garnis**, **saffron**, **salt**, and 2 quarts (2 L) of water. Let cook for 2½ hours over very low heat, covered, or just until the **lamb** is cooked to the desired doneness and the vegetables are tender; serve.

ASIAN-STYLE PORK SPARE RIBS

Pork spare ribs
x 2 slabs (about 2½ lb/1.2 kg total)

Fresh ginger
5¼ ounces (150 g)

Lemongrass
2 stalks

Soy sauce
½ cup (120 mL)

Honey
4 tbsp (60 mL)

Cilantro
1 bunch

Preparation time: 10 min.
Marinating: Overnight
Cooking time: 1 hr.

- The day before, cut the **ribs** into sections. Peel and grate the **ginger**. Finely chop the **lemongrass**.
- Add the **ribs** to a baking dish with the **ginger**, **lemongrass**, **soy sauce**, and **honey**. Refrigerate to marinate overnight.
- The next day, preheat the oven to 350°F/180°C.
- Place the baking dish in the oven and bake for 1 hour, or until the **ribs** are cooked to the desired doneness. Sprinkle with **cilantro** leaves and serve.

SALT PORK IN LENTILS

Pork spare ribs (lightly salted)
x 1 slab (2½ lb/1.2 kg)

Salt pork (lightly salted)
2 lb (900 g)

Bouquets garnis (bay leaf, thyme)
x 2

Chicken bouillon
1 extra-large cube

Green lentils
1⅛ lb (500 g)

👤 6

🧂 **Pepper**

🕐
Preparation time: 5 min.
Desalting: 2 hr.
Cooking time: 2 hr. 5 min.

• Cut the **ribs** and **salt pork** into large pieces. Soak the pieces for 2 hours in cold water, changing the water every 30 minutes.

• Place the **pork** in a heavy pot with the **bouquets garnis**, **bouillon**, and 2 quarts (2 L) of water. Bring to a boil, then cook over low heat, covered, for 1 hour 15 minutes.

• Add the **lentils** and cook over low heat, covered, for 45 more minutes, or until the **pork** is cooked to the desired doneness and the **lentils** are tender. Add pepper; serve.

CORSICAN MEATBALLS

Mint
1 bunch

Baby spinach
5¼ ounces (150 g)

Ground sausage
1⅛ lb (500 g)

Grated Parmesan cheese
1 oz (25 g)

Egg, beaten
x 1

Crushed tomatoes
1 small can (14 ounces/400 g)

Preparation time: 10 min.
Cooking time: 25 min.

- Preheat the oven to 350°F/180°C.
- Chop the **mint** and **spinach**. Using your hands, thoroughly combine the **sausage** with the **mint**, **spinach**, **Parmesan**, and **egg**. Roll the mixture into 10 meatballs.
- Pour the **tomatoes** into a baking dish and add the meatballs. Bake for 25 minutes, or until the meatballs are browned and cooked through; serve.

PORK SHOULDER AND CHANTERELLES

Pork shoulder
2¼ lb (1 kg)

Maple syrup
3 tbsp (45 mL)

Soy sauce
½ cup (120 mL)

**Bouquets garnis
(bay leaf, thyme)**
x 2

**Chanterelle mushrooms
(girolle)**
10½ ounces (300 g)

**Trumpet chanterelle
mushrooms**
7 ounces (200 g)

🧍 6

🧂 **Salt, pepper**

🕐

Preparation time: 5 min.
Marinating: 1 hr.
Cooking time: 1 hr. 15 min.

• Cut the **pork shoulder** into 2 pieces. Marinate it for 1 hour in the **maple syrup**, **soy sauce**, and **bouquets garnis**.
• Transfer the **pork** and the marinade liquid to a large heavy pot and add 1¼ cups (300 mL) of water. Bring to a boil and cook over low heat, covered, for 1 hour, or until the **pork** is cooked to the desired doneness.
• Add the **mushrooms** and cook for 10 more minutes.
• Add salt and pepper. Serve with a side of puréed potatoes, if desired.

ROAST PORK TIAN

Potato
x 1 (medium)

Zucchini
x 1

Tomatoes
x 2

Pork roast, boneless
x 1 (2½ lb/1.2 kg)

**Grated cheese
(such as Gruyère)**
1¾ ounces (50 g)

👤👤👤👤

🧂🧂 **Salt, pepper**

🫗 **Drizzle of extra-virgin olive oil**

🕐

**Preparation time: 15 min.
Cooking time: 45 min.**

- Preheat the oven to 400°F/210°C.
- Thinly slice the **potato**, **zucchini**, and **tomatoes**.
- Make 12 deep incisions crosswise along the top of the **roast**. Tuck the **potato**, **zucchini**, and **tomato** slices into the incisions. Place the **roast** in a baking dish and sprinkle the **cheese** over the top. Add salt and pepper and a drizzle of oil. Bake for 45 minutes, or until the **pork** is cooked to the desired doneness, basting occasionally with the cooking juices; serve.

PORK SHOULDER WITH LEMON

Pork shoulder
1⅓ lb (600 g)

Organic lemon
x 1

Granulated sugar
1 tbsp (½ ounces/13 g)

Soy sauce
½ cup (120 mL)

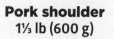

Preparation time: 10 min.
Cooking time: 1 hr.

- Preheat the oven to 350°F/180°C.
- Cut the **pork** into large cubes. Zest the **lemon** in long strips, then juice it.
- Combine the **pork**, **lemon** zest and juice, **sugar**, **soy sauce**, and ⅓ cup (100 mL) of water in a baking dish. Bake for 1 hour, or until the **pork** is cooked to the desired doneness, basting occasionally with the cooking juices (add a little water if it seems dry); serve.

SKILLET SAUSAGE WITH COUSCOUS

Zucchinis
x 2

Tomatoes
x 4

Merguez sausages
x 4

**Ras el hanout
(Moroccan spice blend)**
2 tbsp

Salt, pepper

Preparation time: 5 min.
Cooking time: 15 min.

• Chop the **zucchinis**, **tomatoes**, and **sausages** into large pieces. Place them in a skillet with the **ras el hanout** and 2⅔ cups (600 mL) of water. Add salt and pepper. Bring to a boil and let cook for 10 minutes, or until the **sausage** is cooked through and the vegetables are tender.
• Serve with a side of cooked couscous.

PORK TENDERLOIN WITH PARMESAN AND CILANTRO

Toasted white bread
x 1 slice

Cilantro
1 bunch

Parmesan cheese shavings
1¾ ounces (50 g)

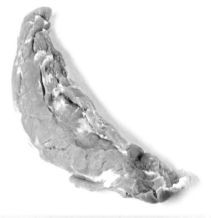

Pork tenderloin
x 1 (about 1½ lb/700 g)

Cherry tomatoes
1 container (9 ounces/250 g)

Salt, pepper

4 tbsp (60 mL) flavorless cooking oil

Preparation time: 5 min.
Cooking time: 40 min.

- Preheat the oven to 400°F/210°C.
- Crush the toasted **bread** into fine crumbs. Chop the **cilantro** leaves (reserving 2 sprigs). Combine the crumbs with the chopped **cilantro**, **Parmesan** shavings, and 2 tbsp (30 mL) of the oil. Salt and pepper the **pork**. Place it in a baking dish drizzled with the remaining 2 tbsp (30 mL) of oil and bake for 20 minutes.
- Spread the crumb mixture on top of the **pork**. Add the **tomatoes** and bake for 20 more minutes. Top the pork with the remaining **cilantro**; serve.

SIMPLE CASSOULET

Toulouse sausage or other fresh pork sausage
x 4

White kidney beans
1 large can (1¾ lb/800 g), drained

Garlic
8 cloves (unpeeled)

Bouquets garnis (bay leaf, thyme)
x 2

Crushed tomatoes
1 small can (14 ounces/400 g)

Toasted white bread
x 2

👤👤👤👤

🧂🧂 **Salt, pepper**

⏱

Preparation time: 5 min.
Cooking time: 40 min.

- Preheat the oven to 350°F/180°C.
- Chop the **sausages**. Place the **sausage** pieces, **beans**, **garlic**, **bouquets garnis**, and **tomatoes** in a large baking dish. Add salt and pepper. Crumble the **toast** over the top and bake for 25 minutes.
- Stir, then bake for 15 more minutes, or until the **sausage** is cooked through. Serve hot.

STEWED RED CABBAGE WITH SAUSAGE

Red cabbage
x ½ head

**Morteau sausage or other
fresh smoked sausage**
x 1

Smoked bacon
2 thick slices

**Bouquets garnis
(bay leaf, thyme)**
x 3

Potatoes
x 4 (medium)

4 to 6

Salt, pepper

Preparation time: 10 min.
Cooking time: 1 hr. 25 min.

- Coarsely chop the **cabbage**. Slice the **sausage** into thick rounds. Halve the **bacon** slices.
- Place the **cabbage**, **sausage**, **bacon**, and **bouquets garnis** in a large heavy pot with 5 cups (1.2 L) of water. Add salt and pepper and cook over low heat, covered, for 1 hour.
- Peel and chop the **potatoes**, then add them to the pot. Cook for 25 more minutes, or until the **sausage** is cooked through and the **potatoes** are tender; serve.

RACK OF PORK IN MUSTARD

Carrots
x 5

Sweet potatoes
x 2

Red onions
x 3

Pork rack
x 1 (10 chops)

Coarse-grain mustard
4 tbsp (60 mL)

**Bouquets garnis
(bay leaf, thyme)**
x 4

 8

🧂🧂 **Salt, pepper**

🫗 **4 tbsp (60 mL)
flavorless cooking oil**

🕐

**Preparation time: 10 min.
Cooking time: 1 hr. 30 min.**

- Preheat the oven to 400°F/210°C.
- Peel and chop the **carrots**, **sweet potatoes**, and **onions**. Place them in a baking dish with the **pork rack**.
- Combine the **mustard** and oil and coat the top of the pork with this mixture. Add the **bouquets garnis** and 1¼ cups (300 mL) of water. Add salt and pepper and bake for 1 hour 30 minutes, or until the **pork** is cooked to the desired doneness and the vegetables are tender; serve.

PORK TENDERLOIN WITH SAGE AND BACON

Pork tenderloin
x 1 (about 1½ lb/700 g)

Bacon
8 thin slices

Sage
10 leaves

👤👤👤👤

🕐

Preparation time: 5 min.
Cooking time: 40 min.
Resting time: 2 min.

- Preheat the oven to 350°F/180°C.
- Wrap the **tenderloin** in the **bacon** and **sage** leaves. Place the **tenderloin** in a baking dish with ⅓ cup (100 mL) of water and bake for 40 minutes, or until the **bacon** is crisped and the **pork** is cooked to the desired doneness.
- Let rest for 2 minutes, then cut into thick portions and serve.

COCONUT AND TARRAGON MUSSELS

Mussels
2 quarts (2 L), cleaned,
beards removed

Coconut milk
1⅔ cups (400 mL)

Tarragon
1 bunch

Preparation time: 5 min.
Cooking time: 5 to 8 min.

• In a large pot over high heat, cook the **mussels** in the **coconut milk** for 5 minutes, stirring, or until the **mussels** open.

• Coarsely chop the **tarragon**.

• Remove from the heat, add the **tarragon**, and stir to combine; serve.

GARLIC BASIL SHRIMP

Raw shrimp
x 20

Garlic powder
2 tsp

Sweetened soy sauce
2 tbsp (30 mL)

Basil
1 bunch

👤👤👤👤

🧂 Salt, pepper

🫗 2 tbsp (30 mL)
flavorless cooking oil

⏲

Preparation time: 5 min.
Marinating: 30 min.
Cooking time: 1 min.

- Peel the **shrimp** and marinate them for 30 minutes in the **garlic powder**, **soy sauce**, and **oil**.
- Just before serving, sauté the **shrimp** in the marinade liquid for 1 minute, while stirring, or just until the **shrimp** are cooked through.
- Remove from the heat, add **basil** leaves, and stir to combine; serve.

LOBSTER IN TOMATO SAUCE

Lobsters
x 2 (raw)

Garlic
1 clove

Cognac
5 tbsp (75 mL)

White wine
½ bottle (375 mL)

Tarragon
5 sprigs

Crushed tomatoes
1 large can (28 oz/800 g)

Salt, pepper

2 tbsp (30 mL)
flavorless cooking oil

Preparation time: 15 min.
Cooking time: 18 min.

- Chop the **lobsters** into 4 pieces each; break the claws using a mallet. Peel and chop the **garlic**.
- In a large heavy pot, cook the **lobster** pieces in the oil for 2 minutes. Add the **cognac**, cook for 1 more minute, then add the **wine**, **garlic**, **tarragon**, and **tomatoes**. Add salt and pepper and let simmer over low heat for 15 minutes, or until the **lobsters** are cooked through; serve.

GARLIC SHRIMP IN SOY SAUCE

Assorted bell peppers
x 2

Garlic
4 cloves

Raw shrimp
9 ounces (250 g)

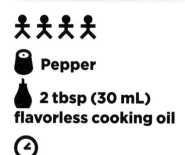

Bean sprouts
14 ounces (400 g)

Soy sauce
4 tbsp (60 mL)

👤👤👤👤

🫙 Pepper

🫗 2 tbsp (30 mL)
flavorless cooking oil

🕐

Preparation time: 10 min.
Cooking time: 11 min.

• Remove the stems and seed the **bell peppers**; thinly slice the flesh. Peel and chop the **garlic**. Peel the **shrimp**.
• In a skillet with the oil, cook the **shrimp**, **bell peppers**, **garlic**, and **bean sprouts** for 8 minutes.
• Add the **soy sauce**, stir to combine, and cook for 3 more minutes, or just until the **shrimp** are cooked through. Add pepper and serve immediately.

MONKFISH CHEEKS BOURGUIGNON

Monkfish cheeks
1⅛ lb (500 g)

Bacon lardons
6⅓ ounces (180 g)

All-purpose flour
1 tbsp (¼ oz/6 g)

Red wine
1 bottle (750 mL)

**Bouquets garnis
(bay leaf, thyme)**
x 2

👤👤👤👤

🧂🧂 Salt, pepper

🫗 **1 tbsp (15 mL)
flavorless cooking oil**

🕐

Preparation time: 5 min.
Cooking time: 45 min.

- In a large heavy pot, sauté the **cheeks** and **lardons** in the **oil** until lightly browned.
- Add the **flour**, **wine**, and **bouquets garnis**. Let cook over low heat, uncovered, for 45 minutes, or until the **cheeks** are cooked through. Add salt and pepper; serve.

SEA BREAM WITH OLIVES AND OREGANO

Tomatoes
x 2

Sea bream (daurade) fillets
x 4

Capers
2 tbsp (1¾ ounces/50 g)

**Black olives
(Greek marinated)**
x 20

Dried oregano
1 tbsp

Extra-virgin olive oil
2 tbsp (30 mL)

Salt, pepper

**Preparation time: 5 min.
Cooking time: 15 min.**

- Preheat the oven to 350°F/180°C.
- Slice the **tomatoes**.
- In a large baking dish, place the **fillets**, **capers**, **olives**, **oregano**, and **oil**. Top with the **tomato** slices. Add salt and pepper. Bake for 15 minutes, or just until the fish is cooked through; serve from the baking dish.

STUFFED MUSSELS

Mussels
x 32 (large), cleaned, beards removed

White wine
Just over ¾ cup (200 mL)

Ground sausage
5½ ounces (160 g)

Crushed tomatoes
1 small can (14 ounces/400 g)

Thyme
2 sprigs

🚶🚶🚶🚶

🧂 **Pepper**

🕐

Preparation time: 20 min.
Cooking time: 25 min.

- Preheat the oven to 350°F/180°C.
- Cook the **mussels** in the **wine** in a large heavy pot for 5 minutes, or just until they open; remove the **mussels** from the pot.
- Tuck a piece of **ground sausage** inside each shell and loosely tie them closed with kitchen twine. Place the **mussels** in a baking dish with the **tomatoes**, **thyme**, pepper, and the cooking juices from the pot. Bake for 20 minutes, or until the **mussels** are cooked through. Serve immediately.

WHOLE SEA BREAM WITH TOMATO

Garlic
3 cloves (unpeeled)

Thyme
1 small bunch

Extra-virgin olive oil
⅔ cup (150 mL)

Assorted tomatoes
2¼ lb (1 kg)

Whole sea bream (daurade)
x 1 (2 lb/900 g)

👤👤👤👤

🧂🧂 **Salt, pepper**

🕐

Preparation time: 5 min.
Infusion time: 30 min.
Cooking time: 30 min.

- Coarsely chop the **garlic**. Place the **thyme** and **garlic** in a saucepan with the **oil**. Cook over low heat for 5 minutes, then set aside off the heat to infuse for 30 minutes.
- Preheat the oven to 400°F/210°C.
- Slice the **tomatoes** and arrange them on the bottom of a baking dish. Place the **fish** on top, add salt and pepper, brush with the infused oil, and bake for 25 minutes, or until the **fish** is cooked through. Serve from the baking dish.

SALMON IN SORREL SAUCE

Salmon fillets
x 4 (about 3 ounces/85 g each),
skin on

Heavy cream
1⅓ cups (330 mL)

Baby spinach
1¾ ounces (50 g)

Sorrel
2 bunches

👤👤👤👤

🧂🧂 **Salt, pepper**

🫗 **Drizzle of extra-virgin olive oil**

🕐

Preparation time: 5 min.
Cooking time: 15 min.

- Preheat the oven to 400°F/210°C.
- Place the **fillets** in a baking dish and bake for 10 minutes, or until cooked to the desired doneness.
- In a saucepan, bring the **cream** to a boil. Add the **spinach** and **sorrel**. Remove from the heat and briefly blend the mixture using an immersion blender. Add salt and pepper.
- Spoon the sauce over the **fillets**. Serve, drizzled with oil.

MACKEREL IN TOMATO AND WHITE WINE

Tomatoes
x 2

White wine
1¼ cups (300 mL)

Rosemary
2 sprigs

Mackerel fillets
x 4 (large) or x 8 (small)

🧂 **Salt, pepper**

🕐

Preparation time: 5 min.
Cooking time: 20 min.

- Preheat the oven to 400°F/210°C.
- Dice the **tomatoes**. In a saucepan, bring the **tomatoes**, **wine**, and **rosemary** to a boil.
- Place the **fillets** in a baking dish and pour the hot mixture over them. Add salt and pepper. Bake for 15 minutes, or until the fillets are cooked through. Let cool slightly and serve.

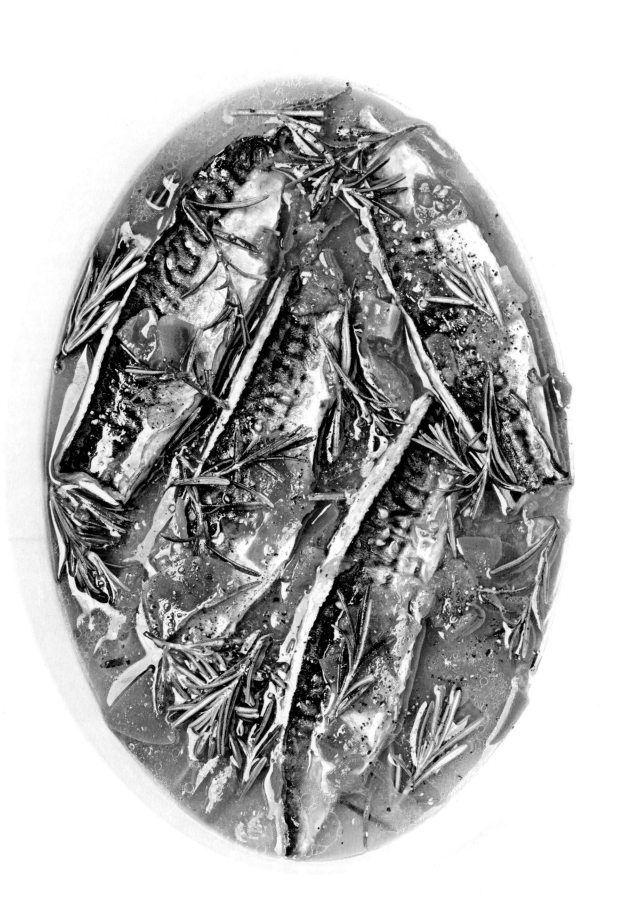

WHITING IN GRAPEFRUIT

Whiting fillets
x 4

Cherry tomatoes
x 20

Frozen peas
9 ounces (250 g), thawed

Extra-virgin olive oil
2 tbsp (30 mL)

Grapefruit juice
⅓ cup (100 mL)

Basil
½ bunch

Salt, pepper

Preparation time: 5 min.
Cooking time: 15 min.

- Preheat the oven to 400°F/210°C.
- Arrange the **fillets** in a baking dish. Halve the **tomatoes**. Add the **tomatoes**, **peas**, **oil**, and **grapefruit juice** to the dish. Add salt and pepper and bake for 15 minutes, or until the **fillets** are cooked through.
- Add **basil** leaves, stir to combine, and serve.

SALT-CRUSTED SEA BASS

Coarse gray salt
1⅛ lb (500 g)

Anise seeds
2 tbsp

Sea bass
x 1 whole (3 lb/1.3 kg),
gutted, not scaled

Heavy cream
Just over ¾ cup (200 mL)

Star anise
x 5

Unsalted butter
7 tbsp (3½ ounces/100 g)

 **Salt, pepper**

Preparation time: 10 min.
Cooking time: 40 min.

- Preheat the oven to 400°F/210°C.
- Combine the **salt** and **anise seeds**. Place the **fish** on a rimmed baking sheet, cover it completely with a thick layer of the salt mixture, and bake for 40 minutes, or until the salt layer has browned slightly and the **fish** is cooked through.
- Meanwhile, in a saucepan, boil the **cream** with the **star anise**. Cook for 20 seconds, stirring, then whisk in the **butter** off the heat. Add salt and pepper.
- Serve the **fish** with the cream sauce.

OCTOPUS COUSCOUS

Carrots
x 2

Turnips
x 3

Celery
2 stalks

Octopus
x 1 small (cleaned and cut up

Ras el hanout
(Moroccan spice blend)
1 tbsp

Canned chickpeas
2⅛ ounces (60 g, drained)

Preparation time: 10 min.
Cooking time: 1 hr.

- Peel and chop the **carrots** and **turnips**. Chop the **celery**.
- In a large pot, place the **octopus**, **carrots**, **turnips**, **celery**, **ras el hanout**, **chickpeas**, and just enough water to cover the ingredients. Simmer for 1 hour over low heat, covered, or until the **octopus** is cooked through.
- Serve with a side of cooked couscous.

BAKED SARDINES WITH HARISSA

Sardines
x 32

Harissa (North African hot pepper paste)
4 tsp (20 mL)

Couscous
4 tbsp (1¾ ounces/50 g)

Extra-virgin olive oil
4 tbsp (60 mL)

Preparation time: 5 min.
Cooking time: 20 min.

- Preheat the oven to 400°F/210°C.
- Place the **sardines** on a baking sheet. Combine the **harissa**, **couscous**, and **oil** and coat the **sardines** with this mixture. Bake for 20 minutes, or just until the **sardines** are cooked through; serve.

CODFISH WITH MUSTARD EN PAPILLOTE

Tomato
x 1

Codfish fillet
x 1 (1¾ lb/800 g)

Coarse-grain mustard
2 tbsp (30 mL)

Tarragon
4 sprigs

Salt, pepper

Preparation time: 10 min.
Cooking time: 15 min.

- Preheat the oven to 400°F/210°C.
- Slice the **tomato**.
- Cut the **fillet** into 4 pieces and place each piece on a small square of parchment paper. Top each with the **mustard**, a **tomato** slice, and a **tarragon** sprig. Add salt and pepper. Gather up the edges of the parchment and fold them tightly to seal. Bake for 15 minutes, or just until the fish is cooked through; serve.

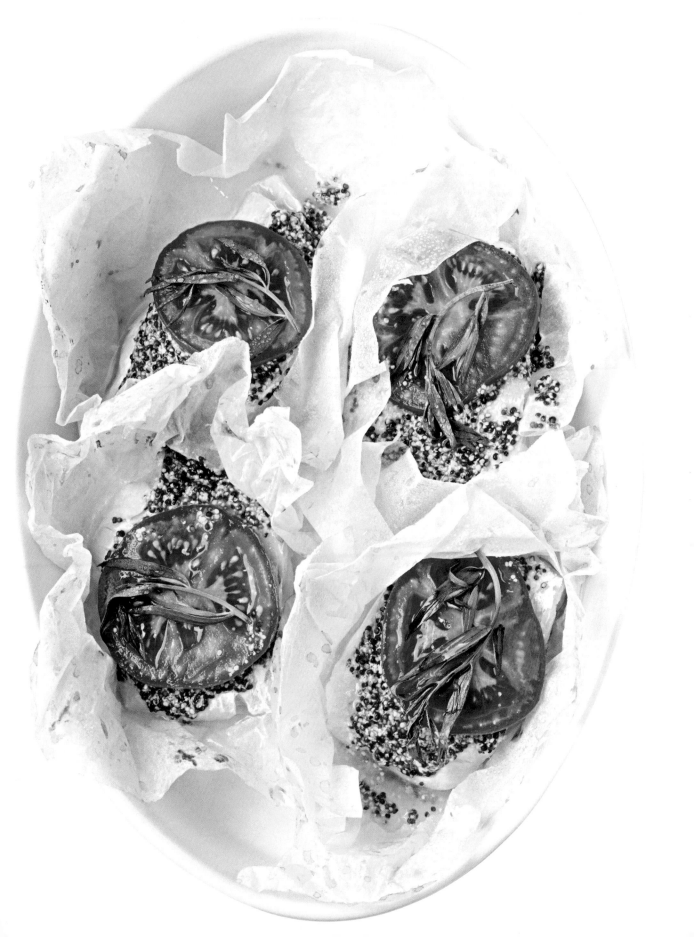

SALMON WITH PARMESAN-TARRAGON BUTTER CRUMB TOPPING

All-purpose flour
1 cup (3½ ounces/100 g)

Unsalted butter
7 tbsp (3½ ounces/100 g),
at room temperature

Dried tarragon
1 tbsp

Parmesan cheese shavings
3½ ounces (100 g)

Salmon fillets
x 4 (about 3 ounces/85 g each),
skin on

Preparation time: 5 min.
Cooking time: 15 min.

- Preheat the oven to 350°F/180°C.
- Combine the **flour**, **butter**, **tarragon**, and **Parmesan** to form a crumbly topping.
- Place the **fillets** in a baking dish, cover them with the topping, then bake for 15 minutes, or just until the **fillets** are cooked to the desired doneness. Serve hot.

BEER-BATTERED FISH

Codfish fillets
x 1 (1¾ lb/800 g), boned

Eggs
x 2 (separated)

All-purpose flour
1 cup (3½ ounces/100 g)

Beer
⅓ cup (100 mL)

**Mixed herbs (dill, chives,
mint, parsley)**
1 bunch

Mayonnaise
4 tbsp (60 mL)

Oil, for deep frying

**Preparation time: 15 min.
Cooking time: 8 min.**

- Cut the **fillets** into 8 pieces. Using an electric mixer, beat the **egg** whites into stiff peaks.
- In a bowl, combine the **flour**, **beer**, and the **egg** yolks, then fold in the beaten **egg** whites to form a batter.
- In a heavy pot, heat 1½ inches of oil until hot. Dredge the fish pieces in the batter until well coated, then carefully lower them into the hot oil and fry, 4 pieces at a time, for 8 minutes, or until browned.
- Chop the **herbs**, stir them into the **mayonnaise**, and serve with the fried fish.

DECADENT CHOCOLATE CAKE

Granulated sugar
1 cup (7 ounces/200 g)

Eggs
x 6 (separated)

All-purpose flour
5 tsp (⅓ oz/10 g)

Unsalted butter
14 tbsp (7 ounces/200 g)

Dark chocolate
7 ounces/200 g + 4 squares
for grating

**Preparation time: 15 min.
Cooking time: 40 min.**

Unmold the cake while it's still warm, let cool, then grate chocolate over the top. Enjoy warm or cooled.

- Preheat the oven to 325°F/160°C. In a bowl, whisk half the **sugar** with the **egg** yolks until lightened. Whisk in the **flour**.
- Melt the **butter** with the **chocolate** over a bain-marie until smooth (or microwave 3 minutes). Stir this into the flour mixture.
- Using an electric mixer, beat the **egg** whites into stiff peaks, sprinkle in the remaining **sugar**, then beat for 5 seconds more. Fold the **egg** whites into the chocolate mixture.
- Scrape the batter into a greased 8-inch (20-cm) cake pan. Bake for 40 minutes, or until a toothpick inserted in the center comes out with a few moist crumbs.

CANTALOUPE AND STRAWBERRY FRUIT SALAD

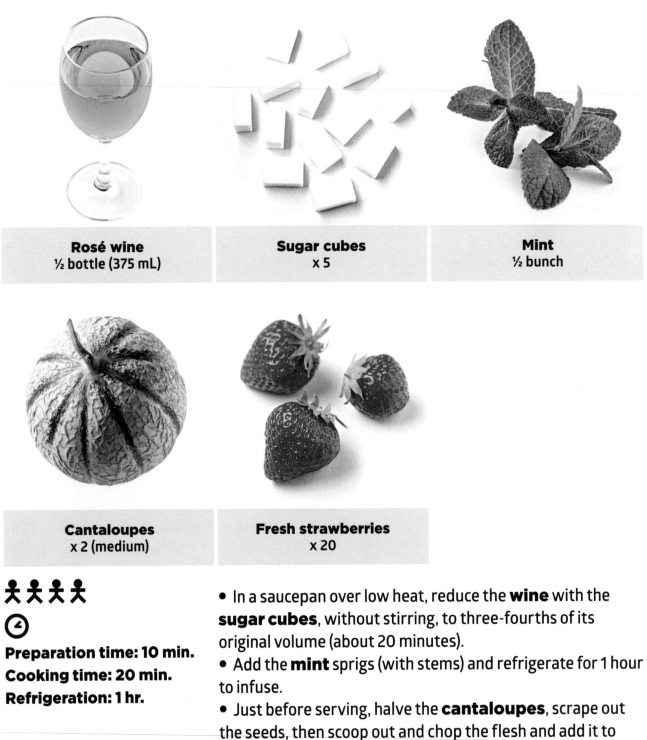

Rosé wine
½ bottle (375 mL)

Sugar cubes
x 5

Mint
½ bunch

Cantaloupes
x 2 (medium)

Fresh strawberries
x 20

Preparation time: 10 min.
Cooking time: 20 min.
Refrigeration: 1 hr.

- In a saucepan over low heat, reduce the **wine** with the **sugar cubes**, without stirring, to three-fourths of its original volume (about 20 minutes).
- Add the **mint** sprigs (with stems) and refrigerate for 1 hour to infuse.
- Just before serving, halve the **cantaloupes**, scrape out the seeds, then scoop out and chop the flesh and add it to the pan with the syrup. Hull and quarter the **strawberries** and add them to the pan. Transfer the mixture to the empty **cantaloupe** halves and serve.

CHOCOLATE WALNUT BROWNIES

Dark chocolate
8½ ounces (240 g)

Walnut halves
x 20

Unsalted butter
10 tbsp (5¼ ounces/150 g)

All-purpose flour
9 tbsp (2⅛ ounces/60 g)

Eggs
x 2

Preparation time: 5 min.
Cooking time: 13 min.

- Preheat the oven to 400°F/210°C.
- Chop the **chocolate** and **walnut halves**.
- Gently melt the **butter** with the **chocolate** over a bain-marie until smooth (or microwave for 3 minutes in a microwave-safe bowl). Whisk in the **flour**.
- Using an electric mixer, beat the **eggs** until lightened. Stir the **eggs** into the chocolate mixture, then fold in the **walnuts**. Scrape the batter into an 8 by 8-inch (20 by 20-cm) baking pan lined with greased parchment paper. Bake for 10 minutes; let cool completely in the pan and serve.

APPLE CINNAMON STRUDEL

Pie crust dough
x 2 sheets (8 ounces/227 g each)

Apples
x 4

Granulated sugar
4 tbsp (1¾ ounces/50 g)

Cinnamon
2 tsp

Unsalted butter
3 tbsp (1¾ ounces/50 g),
at room temperature

Preparation time: 10 min.
Cooking time: 40 min.

- Preheat the oven to 350°F/180°C.
- Unroll the **dough** sheets. Peel, core, and chop the **apples**.
- Unroll one of the **dough** sheets and arrange the **apples** on top, then sprinkle on half of both the **sugar** and the **cinnamon**. Place the other **dough** sheet on top, form into a log, then pinch the **dough** closed.
- Place the strudel on a baking sheet, distribute small pieces of the **butter** over the top, then sprinkle with the remaining **sugar** and **cinnamon**. Bake for 40 minutes, or until golden; let cool and serve.

CLASSIC TIRAMISU

Eggs
x 3 (separated)

Granulated sugar
3 tbsp (1½ ounces/40 g)

Mascarpone cheese
9 ounces (250 g)

Ladyfinger cookies
x 18

Espresso coffee
⅓ cup (100 mL), chilled

Unsweetened cocoa powder
2 tbsp (⅓ oz/10 g)

Preparation time: 30 min.
Refrigeration: 2 hr.
Dust with cocoa; serve.

- Whisk the **egg** yolks with the **sugar** until lightened. Whisk in the **mascarpone**.
- Using an electric mixer, beat the **egg** whites into stiff peaks, then fold them into the yolk mixture.
- Briefly dip the **cookies** in the **espresso** and line half of them in the bottom of a serving dish with high sides. Add a layer of the mascarpone mixture, then another layer of soaked cookies. Refrigerate for 2 hours to chill; serve.

APPLE CRISP

Puff pastry dough
x 1 sheet (8 ounces/227 g)

Apples
x 2 (large)

Unsalted butter
5 tbsp (2½ ounces/75 g),
at room temperature

Granulated sugar
5 tbsp (2¼ ounces/63 g)

☆☆☆☆

🧂 **Confectioners' sugar**

🕑

Preparation time: 5 min.
Cooking time: 40 min.

- Preheat the oven to 350°F/180°C.
- Unroll the **dough** onto a parchment-lined baking sheet. Core and thinly slice the **apples**. Distribute the **apples** on top of the **dough** to about 1 inch (3 cm) from the edge. Distribute small pieces of the **butter** on top, then sprinkle the entire surface with the **sugar**.
- Bake for 40 minutes, or until the **apples** are tender and the edges are puffed and browned. Dust with confectioners' sugar; serve.

LEMON LOAF CAKE

All-purpose flour
2 cups (7 ounces/200 g)

Confectioners' sugar
½ cup (3½ ounces/100 g) + 10 tbsp
(2⅛ ounces/60 g)

Baking powder
1¼ tsp (⅛ oz/5 g)

Organic lemons
x 3

Unsalted butter
14 tbsp (7 ounces/200 g)

Eggs
x 3

👤 **4 to 5**

🕐

Preparation time: 10 min.
Cooking time: 25 min.
Resting time: 10 min.

The glaze will spread over the cooled cake.

- Preheat the oven to 350°F/180°C.
- Whisk together the **flour**, ½ cup (3½ ounces/100 g) of the **confectioners' sugar**, and the **baking powder**.
- Zest and juice 2 of the **lemons**. In a saucepan, melt the **butter** with the zest and juice. Lightly beat the **eggs** with a fork, then add them to the pan. Combine the two mixtures, then scrape into a greased 9½-inch (24-cm) loaf pan and bake for 25 minutes. Let cool
- Combine the remaining **confectioners' sugar** and the juice of the remaining **lemon** until smooth. Pour the glaze over the cake, and let sit for 10 minutes.

BERRY AND WATERMELON FRUIT SALAD

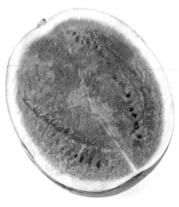

Watermelon wedge
7 ounces (200 g)

Fresh strawberries
1 container (9 ounces/250 g)

Mixed fresh berries
3 containers (13¼ ounces/375 g)

Organic limes
x 2

Confectioners' sugar
4 tbsp (1 oz/25 g)

Preparation time: 10 min.
Refrigeration time: 15 min.

- Cut up the **watermelon** flesh. Hull and quarter the **strawberries**.
- Combine all the **berries** and the **watermelon** in a serving dish. Zest and juice the **limes** and stir this into the fruit mixture with the **confectioners' sugar**. Refrigerate for 15 minutes, or until chilled.
- Stir gently to combine; serve.

NEVER-FAIL TARTE TATIN

Apples
x 6

Unsalted butter
2½ tbsp (1½ ounces/40 g)

Granulated sugar
6 tbsp (2½ ounces/75 g)

Puff pastry dough
x 1 sheet (8 ounces/227 g)

Preparation time: 10 min.
Cooking time: 40 min.

- Preheat the oven to 350°F/180°C.
- Peel, core, and quarter the **apples**. Sauté them for 5 minutes in a skillet with the **butter** and **sugar**, or until slightly softened.
- Line an 8-inch (20-cm) tart pan with the **dough**, arrange the **apples** on top in a single layer, then press them down gently with a spoon. Bake for 35 minutes, or until the edges are golden and the **apples** tender. Serve warm or cooled.

CRÈME CARAMEL

Sugar cubes
x 25

Eggs
x 8 (5 whole + 3 yolks)

Granulated sugar
1 cup (7 ounces/200 g)

Vanilla bean
1 pod

Whole milk
4¼ cups (1 L)

Preparation time: 10 min.
Cooking time: 1 hr. 15 min.
Refrigeration: Overnight
Refrigerate overnight to set.
Unmold and serve sliced.

- Preheat the oven to 300°F/150°C.
- In a heavy-bottom saucepan, melt the **sugar cubes** with 3 tbsp (45 mL) of water until amber in color, then pour the caramel into a 9-inch (23-cm) loaf pan. Whisk together the **whole eggs**, **egg yolks**, and **granulated sugar**.
- Split the **vanilla bean** and scrape the seeds into saucepan with the **milk** and empty pod. Bring to a boil, then pour the hot **milk** into the egg mixture while whisking vigorously; remove the pod. Scrape the mixture into the pan. Bake for 1 hour in a bain-marie.

DARK CHOCOLATE MOUSSE

| **Dark chocolate** | **Eggs** |
| 7 ounces (200 g) | x 6 (separated) |

♟♟♟♟

Preparation time: 10 min.
Cooking time: 5 min.
Refrigeration: 2 hr.

• Chop the **chocolate**, then gently melt it over a bain-marie until smooth (or microwave for 3 minutes in a microwave-safe bowl); let cool slightly. Whisk in the **egg** yolks.
• Using an electric mixer, beat the **egg** whites into stiff peaks, then fold them into the chocolate mixture.
• Divide the mousse among 4 ramekins and refrigerate for 2 hours, or until set; serve.

APRICOT AND ALMOND FREE-FORM TART

Apricots
x 6

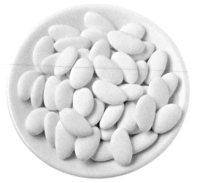

Jordan almonds
x 20

Pie crust dough
x 1 sheet (8 ounces/227 g)

Granulated sugar
2 tbsp (1 oz/25 g)

👤👤👤👤

🕐

Preparation time: 5 min.
Cooking time: 25 min.

- Preheat the oven to 350°F/180°C.
- Pit and quarter the **apricots**. Crush the **almonds**.
- Unroll the **dough** sheet onto a parchment-lined baking sheet. Distribute the **apricots**, then the **almonds**, on top, leaving about a 2-inch (5-cm) border. Fold up the edges to cover part of the filling. Sprinkle with the **sugar** and bake for 25 minutes, or until the edges are golden and the **apricots** tender; serve.

CHOCOLATE MILLEFEUILLE

Puff pastry dough
x 1 sheet (8 ounces/227 g)

Granulated sugar
4 tbsp (1¾ ounces/50 g)

Heavy cream
1⅓ cups (330 mL), well chilled

Mascarpone cheese
1 tbsp (1¾ ounces/50 g),
well chilled

Unsweetened cocoa powder
6 tbsp (1 oz/30 g)

Preparation time: 15 min.
Cooking time: 12 min.
Dust with the remaining cocoa powder.

- Preheat the oven to 350°F/180°C.
- Roll out the **dough** on a parchment-lined baking sheet. Sprinkle with 3 tbsp (1½ ounces/40 g) of the **sugar** and bake for 12 minutes.
- Meanwhile, combine the **cream** and **mascarpone**. Using an electric mixer, beat the mixture with 4 tbsp (⅔ oz/20 g) of the **cocoa powder** and the remaining **sugar** for about 20 seconds, or until it holds soft peaks.
- Cut the pastry into 3 even rectangles. Layer the cream between the layers of pastry; serve.

PEACHES IN WINE SAUCE

Yellow peaches
x 4

Star anise
x 8

Sugar cubes
x 20

Red wine
1 bottle (750 mL)

Preparation time: 5 min.
Cooking time: 20 min.
Refrigeration: 2 hr.

• Score the skin of the **peaches** and place them in a saucepan with the **star anise**, **sugar cubes**, and **wine**. Bring to a boil and cook for 15 minutes over low heat, or until softened.

• Transfer the **peaches** to a serving dish with the liquid. Refrigerate for 2 hours to cool; serve.

CHOCOLATE AND COCONUT–DIPPED CHERRIES

Dark chocolate
About ½ tablet (3½ ounces/100 g)

Cherries (with stems)
x 20

Grated coconut
6 tbsp (1 oz/30 g)

Preparation time: 5 min.
Cooking time: 1 min.
Refrigeration: 30 min.

- Chop the **chocolate**, then gently melt it over a bain-marie until smooth (or microwave for 1 minute in a microwave-safe bowl).
- Dip the **cherries** into the **chocolate**, then dredge them in the **coconut**. Arrange them on a plate. Refrigerate for 30 minutes, or until set; serve.

CHOCOLATE-MINT CORNFLAKE COOKIES

Dark chocolate
About ½ tablet (3½ ounces/100 g)

Mint
10 leaves

Cornflakes
4½ ounces (125 g)

Preparation time: 5 min.
Cooking time: 1 min.
Refrigeration: 1 hr.

- Chop the **chocolate**, then gently melt it over a bain-marie until smooth (or microwave for 1 minute in a microwave-safe bowl); let cool slightly.
- Chop the **mint**. Thoroughly stir the **cornflakes** and **mint** into the **chocolate** until well coated.
- Spoon the mixture into mounds about 2 inches (5 cm) in diameter onto a parchment-lined tray. Refrigerate for 1 hour, or until set; serve.

INDEX BY INGREDIENT

CHEESE, CUMIN GOUDA
Sauerkraut and Kielbasa Flatbread **140**

CHEESE, FETA
Bell Peppers Stuffed with Feta and Tomato **154**

CHEESE, FROMAGE FRAIS
Sardine and Basil Spread **14**

CHEESE, GOAT
Baked Goat Cheese–Tomato Toasts **60**
Eggplant and Goat Cheese Spread **44**
Goat Cheese and Basil Ravioli **92**
Goat Cheese Pinwheels **8**
Goat Cheese–Zucchini Pockets **58**
Tomatoes Stuffed with Goat Cheese **148**
  and Prosciutto
Zucchini and Fennel Sauté **160**
Zucchini and Goat Cheese Tart **122**

CHEESE, GRATED
Cheese Soufflé **188**
Eggplant Parmigiana **186**
Endive and Chorizo Gratin **162**
Microwave Scalloped Potatoes **176**
Moussaka **166**
Peasant Soup **82**
Potato and Zucchini Gratin **146**
Roast Pork Tian **288**
Scalloped Ham and Leeks **178**
Scalloped Potatoes with Andouille **182**
Vegetable Pizza **130**

CHEESE, MASCARPONE
Chocolate Millefeuille **362**
Classic Tiramisu **346**

CHEESE, MOZZARELLA
Baked Chorizo and Mozzarella Eggplants **150**
Baked Italian-Style Tomatoes **164**
Bell Pepper, Mozzarella, and Tuna Pocket **144**
Cheesy Tuna Pasta Casserole **108**
Eggplant Parmigiana **186**
Fresh Tomato and Basil Pizza **138**
Italian-Style Turkey Cutlets **230**
Lime and Rosemary Chicken **246**
Zucchini and Prosciutto Lasagna **96**

CHEESE, PARMESAN
Asparagus Risotto **116**
Asparagus Twists with Orange Dip **20**
Baked Asparagus with Parmesan- **62**
  Butter Crumb Topping

Baked Coppa Ham Potatoes **172**
Baked Gnocchi Arrabbiata **110**
Baked Vegetables Provençal **174**
Chicken Roulades à l'Orange **238**
Chorizo Sablés **16**
Corsican Meatballs **284**
Cream of Celery Soup with Parmesan **68**
Hawaiian Pizza **136**
Italian-Style Turkey Cutlets **230**
Parmesan Sweet Potato Fries **152**
Pear, Chorizo, and Parmesan Pizza **128**
Pork Tenderloin with Parmesan **294**
  and Cilantro
Prosciutto and Parmesan Bites **18**
Quick Penne Arrabbiata **104**
Rosemary Breadsticks **12**
Salmon with Parmesan-Tarragon **334**
  Butter Crumb Topping
Sausage and Parmesan Pizza **126**
Winter Squash and Meatball Flatbread **134**
Zucchini and Prosciutto Lasagna **96**

CHEESE, REBLOCHON
Apple and Cheese Pizza **132**

CHERRIES
Chocolate and Coconut–Dipped Cherries **366**

CHERRIES, SOUR
Foie Gras Ravioli and Cherry Soup **88**

CHICKEN
Asian Chicken Noodle Soup **86**
Baked Crispy Chicken Drumsticks **228**
Chicken and Olive Spread **22**
Chicken and Peanut Dumplings **190**
Chicken Paella **118**
Chicken Roulades à l'Orange **238**
Chicken with Olives **244**
Coconut and Pesto Chicken **232**
Coconut, Saffron, and Basil Chicken **222**
Ginger Chicken **236**
Lime and Rosemary Chicken **246**
Mango-Curry Chicken **242**
Sweet and Sour Chicken Wings **234**
Whole Roast Chicken on Bread **248**

CHICKPEAS
Octopus Couscous **328**

CHOCOLATE, DARK
Chocolate and Coconut–Dipped Cherries **366**

Chocolate-Mint Cornflake Cookies **368**
Chocolate Walnut Brownies **342**
Dark Chocolate Mousse **358**
Decadent Chocolate Cake **338**

CHORIZO
Baked Chorizo and Mozzarella Eggplants **150**
Baked Gnocchi Arrabbiata **110**
Chicken Paella **118**
Chorizo Pipérade **180**
Chorizo Sablés **16**
Endive and Chorizo Gratin **162**
Hawaiian Pizza **136**
Pear, Chorizo, and Parmesan Pizza **128**
Quick Penne Arrabbiata **104**

CILANTRO
Asian-Style Pork Spare Ribs **280**
Asian-Style Veal Roulades **258**
Beef Sautéed with Lemongrass **192**
Clams with Cilantro and Tomato **66**
Creamy Mushroom Soup with Lardons **78**
Eggplant and Goat Cheese Spread **44**
Ginger Chicken **236**
Mango-Curry Chicken **242**
Mexican Tuna Tartare **52**
Oysters with Avocado and Peppercorns **32**
Pork Tenderloin with Parmesan **294**
  and Cilantro

CLAMS
Clams with Cilantro and Tomato **66**
Clams with Raspberry **28**

COCOA POWDER
Chocolate Millefeuille **362**
Classic Tiramisu **346**
Leg of Venison in Wine Sauce **212**

COCONUT, GRATED
Chocolate and Coconut–Dipped Cherries **366**

COFFEE
Classic Tiramisu **346**

COGNAC
Lobster in Tomato Sauce **308**
Microwave Spiced Foie Gras **26**

CORNFLAKES
Baked Crispy Chicken Drumsticks **228**
Chocolate-Mint Cornflake Cookies **368**

K

KIELBASA
Sauerkraut and Kielbasa Flatbread — 140

L

LADYFINGERS
Classic Tiramisu — 346

LAMB
Colombo Spice Lamb — 274
Curried Lamb Chops — 270
Four-Hour Leg of Lamb — 268
Lamb Shanks in Honey — 276
Lamb Shanks with Citrus — 272
Stewed Leg of Lamb with Saffron — 278

LEEKS
Peasant Soup — 82
Scalloped Ham and Leeks — 178

LEMONS
Lemon Loaf Cake — 350
Mexican Tuna Tartare — 52
Octopus Antipasto — 48
Oysters with Avocado and Peppercorns — 32
Pork Shoulder with Lemon — 290
Sardine and Basil Spread — 14
Tuna-Blueberry Carpaccio — 38

LEMONS, PRESERVED
Four-Hour Leg of Lamb — 268
Mediterranean-Style Stuffed Chile Peppers — 158

LEMONGRASS
Asian Chicken Noodle Soup — 86
Asian-Style Pork Spare Ribs — 280
Asian-Style Veal Roulades — 258
Beef Cheeks with Lemongrass — 204
Beef Sautéed with Lemongrass — 192
Pastrami Spring Rolls — 10
Quick Thai Soup — 84
Thai-Style Beef Tartare — 194
Tomato and Mint Salad — 46
Tomatoes Stuffed with Sausage and Lemongrass — 184
Vietnamese Egg Roll Salad — 50

LIMES
Berry and Watermelon Fruit Salad — 352
Lime and Rosemary Chicken — 246
Salmon Ceviche with Coconut and Basil — 36
Spaghetti with Sardines — 102
Veal Breast in Honey and Lime — 262

LOBSTER
Lobster in Tomato Sauce — 308

M

MACKEREL, CANNED OR FRESH
Mackerel in Tomato and White Wine — 322
Mackerel-In-Mustard Dip — 6

MANGOS
Mango-Curry Chicken — 242
Shrimp and Mango Salad — 56

MAPLE SYRUP
Pork Shoulder and Chanterelles — 286

MELONS
Cantaloupe and Strawberry Fruit Salad — 340
Prosciutto, Cantaloupe, and Arugula Salad — 42
Tomato, Cantaloupe, and Strawberry Gazpacho — 74

MILK
Cheese Soufflé — 188
Crème Caramel — 356

MILK, COCONUT
Coconut and Pesto Chicken — 232
Coconut and Tarragon Mussels — 304
Coconut, Saffron, and Basil Chicken — 222
Mango-Curry Chicken — 242
Orange-Coconut Seafood Soup — 70
Pea and Prosciutto Velouté — 72
Quick Thai Soup — 84
Salmon Ceviche with Coconut and Basil — 36

MINT
Cantaloupe and Strawberry Fruit Salad — 340
Chocolate-Mint Cornflake Cookies — 368
Corsican Meatballs — 284
Curried Lamb Chops — 270
Goat Cheese–Zucchini Pockets — 58
Salmon Ceviche with Passion Fruit — 40
Shrimp and Watermelon Soup — 80
Shrimp Spring Rolls — 30
Strawberry Tabbouleh — 54
Tomato and Mint Salad — 46
Vietnamese Egg Roll Salad — 50

MUSHROOMS, CHANTERELLE
Pork Shoulder and Chanterelles — 286
Venison and Chanterelles — 210

MUSHROOMS, WHITE BUTTON
Creamy Mushroom Soup with Lardons — 78
Pheasant Stew — 218
Quick Thai Soup — 84
Vegetable Pizza — 130

MUSSELS
Chicken Paella — 118
Coconut and Tarragon Mussels — 304
Mussels with Garlic and Parsley — 64
Stuffed Mussels — 316

O

OCTOPUS
Octopus Antipasto — 48
Octopus Couscous — 328

OLIVES, BLACK
Duck Confit Provençal — 252
Sea Bream with Olives and Oregano — 314
Spaghetti with Puttanesca Sauce — 98

OLIVES, GREEN
Four-Hour Leg of Lamb — 268

OLIVES, TAPENADE
Chicken and Olive Spread — 22
Chicken with Olives — 244
Duck Legs with Turnips and Olives — 254
Tuna and Olive Pasta Salad — 94

ONIONS, RED
Quail Bourguignon — 214
Rack of Pork in Mustard — 300
Sausage and Parmesan Pizza — 126

ONIONS, SWEET
Baked Rabbit with Rosemary and Tomatoes — 220
Chorizo Pipérade — 180
Prosciutto-Wrapped Guinea Hens with Potatoes — 240

ORANGES
Asparagus Twists with Orange Dip — 20
Duck Breasts à l'Orange — 256
Lamb Shanks with Citrus — 272
Shrimp and Watermelon Soup — 80

ORANGE JUICE
Chicken Roulades à l'Orange — 238
Orange-Coconut Seafood Soup — 70

OYSTERS
Oysters with Avocado and Peppercorns — 32
Oysters with Foie Gras — 24

P

PASSION FRUIT
Salmon Ceviche with Passion Fruit — 40

S

SAFFRON
Chicken Paella — 118
Coconut, Saffron, and Basil Chicken — 222
Scallop and Saffron Penne — 112
Scallop Risotto — 120
Stewed Leg of Lamb with Saffron — 279

SALMON
Salmon and Ravioli Soup — 90
Salmon Ceviche with Coconut and Basil — 36
Salmon Ceviche with Passion Fruit — 40
Salmon in Sorrel Sauce — 320
Salmon with Parmesan-Tarragon Butter Crumb Topping — 334

SANDWICH BREAD
Baked Goat Cheese–Tomato Toasts — 60

SARDINES
Baked Sardines with Harissa — 330
Sardine and Basil Spread — 14
Spaghetti with Sardines — 102

SAUERKRAUT
Sauerkraut and Kielbasa Flatbread — 140

SAUSAGE, ANDOUILLE
Scalloped Potatoes with Andouille — 182

SAUSAGE, CHIPOLATA
Sausage and Parmesan Pizza — 126

SAUSAGE, GROUND
Corsican Meatballs — 284
Egg and Meatball Ratatouille — 170
Mediterranean-Style Stuffed Chile Peppers — 158
Stuffed Mussels — 316
Tomatoes Stuffed with Sausage and Lemongrass — 184
Winter Squash and Meatball Flatbread — 134

SAUSAGE, MERGUEZ
Skillet Sausage with Couscous — 292

SAUSAGE, MORTEAU
Stewed Red Cabbage with Sausage — 298

SAUSAGE, SMOKED
Sausage and Penne Pasta — 100

SAUSAGE, TOULOUSE
Simple Cassoulet — 296

SCALLOPS
Orange-Coconut Seafood Soup — 70
Scallop and Saffron Penne — 112
Scallop Risotto — 120
Scallop Tagliatelle — 106

SESAME SEEDS
Thai-Style Beef Tartare — 194

SHALLOTS
Pheasant Stew — 218
Rib Eye Steak in Red Wine and Shallot Sauce — 206
Tomato and Mint Salad — 46
Whole Roast Chicken on Bread — 248

SHRIMP
Garlic Basil Shrimp — 306
Garlic Shrimp in Soy Sauce — 310
Orange-Coconut Seafood Soup — 70
Shrimp and Mango Salad — 56
Shrimp and Watermelon Soup — 80
Shrimp Spring Rolls — 30

SHRIMP CHIPS
Shrimp and Mango Salad — 56

SORREL
Salmon in Sorrel Sauce — 320

SPINACH, BABY
Corsican Meatballs — 284
Ham and Spinach Pizza with Mustard — 142
Salmon in Sorrel Sauce — 320
Seared Veal Chop in Tarragon Cream — 260
Spaghetti with Sardines — 102

SPROUTS
Garlic Shrimp in Soy Sauce — 310

SQUASH, BUTTERNUT
Winter Squash and Meatball Flatbread — 134

SQUID
Squid-Ink Paella — 114

SQUID INK
Squid-Ink Paella — 114

STRAWBERRIES
Berry and Watermelon Fruit Salad — 352
Cantaloupe and Strawberry Fruit Salad — 340
Strawberry Tabbouleh — 54
Tomato, Cantaloupe, and Strawberry Gazpacho — 74

SWEET POTATOES
Parmesan Sweet Potato Fries — 152
Rack of Pork in Mustard — 300

T

TARRAGON
Coconut and Tarragon Mussels — 304
Codfish with Mustard en Papillote — 332
Cooked Rabbit Terrine — 216

Lobster in Tomato Sauce — 308
Mackerel-in-Mustard Dip — 6
Salmon with Parmesan-Tarragon Butter Crumb Topping — 334
Seared Veal Chop in Tarragon Cream — 260

TOMATOES
Baked Goat Cheese–Tomato Toasts — 60
Baked Italian-Style Tomatoes — 164
Baked Rabbit with Rosemary and Tomatoes — 220
Baked Vegetables Provençal — 174
Bell Peppers Stuffed with Feta and Tomato — 154
Chicken with Olives — 244
Codfish with Mustard en Papillote — 332
Curried Lamb Chops — 270
Duck Confit Provençal — 252
Egg and Meatball Ratatouille — 170
Eggplant Parmigiana — 186
Italian-Style Turkey Cutlets — 230
Mackerel in Tomato and White Wine — 322
Quick Penne Arrabbiata — 104
Roast Pork Tian — 288
Sea Bream with Olives and Oregano — 314
Skillet Sausage with Couscous — 292
Tomato, Cantaloupe, and Strawberry Gazpacho — 74
Tomatoes Stuffed with Goat Cheese and Prosciutto — 148
Tomatoes Stuffed with Sausage and Lemongrass — 184
Whole Sea Bream with Tomato — 318

TOMATOES, CHERRY
Asparagus Minestrone — 76
Clams with Cilantro and Tomato — 66
Fresh Tomato and Basil Pizza — 138
Orange-Coconut Seafood Soup — 70
Pork Tenderloin with Parmesan and Cilantro — 294
Tomato and Mint Salad — 46
Whiting in Grapefruit — 324

TOMATOES, CRUSHED
Baked Gnocchi Arrabbiata — 110
Corsican Meatballs — 284
Hamburger Pizza — 124
Hawaiian Pizza — 136
Lobster in Tomato Sauce — 308
Mediterranean-Style Stuffed Chile Peppers — 158
Moussaka — 166
Quick Penne Arrabbiata — 104
Sausage and Penne Pasta — 100

Black Dog & Leventhal Publishers
Hachette Book Group
1290 Avenue of the Americas
New York, NY 10104

www.hachettebookgroup.com
www.blackdogandleventhal.com

Originally published as *Simplissime le Livre de Cuisine: Le + Facile du Monde* in 2017 by Hachette Livre in France.

First U.S. edition: September 2018

Black Dog & Leventhal Publishers is an imprint of Running Press, a division of Hachette Book Group. The Black Dog & Leventhal Publishers name and logo are trademarks of Hachette Book Group, Inc.

The publisher is not responsible for websites (or their content) that are not owned by the publisher.

The Hachette Speakers Bureau provides a wide range of authors for speaking events. To find out more, go to www.HachetteSpeakersBureau.com or call (866) 376-6591.

Print book interior design by Marie-Paule Jaulme.

Library of Congress Catalog Number: 2018932216

ISBNs: 978-0-316-44866-6 (hardcover), 978-0-7624-6579-8 (ebook)

Printed in China

IM

10 9 8 7 6 5 4 3 2 1